For thousands of years, until replaced by the railroads and the automobiles, horses were useful as a fast and sure means of transportation.

In this nuclear age, in the majority of countries, horses and ponies are now obsolete in warfare, replaced on land and superseded as transport. Yet all over the world more and more adults and children are learning to ride. Equine sports like show jumping are enormously popular, trekking is a growing pastime and horse breeding and racing are big business. Societies like the Pony and Riding Clubs continue to expand.

Despite the gloomy predictions of a few years ago, horses play an increasing part in modern life. While the number of heavy horses decreases, more 'all purpose' horses are being bred. Types are modified to suit local conditions, and many 'breeds' are really variations of similar kinds. Whether people are concerned with the most valuable thoroughbreds or the humblest family ponies, they share a common desire—the need, in this modern world of man-made machines, to maintain dealings with these striking flesh and blood creatures.

A
GROSSET
ALL COLOR GUIDE

HORSES AND PONIES

BY JUDITH CAMPBELL
Illustrated by Dugald McDougal

GROSSET & DUNLAP
A NATIONAL GENERAL COMPANY
Publishers • New York

CONTENTS

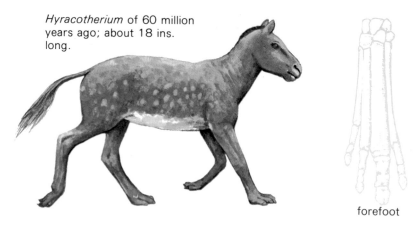

Hyracotherium of 60 million years ago; about 18 ins. long.

forefoot

Miohippus of 30 million years ago; about 4 ft. long.

forefoot

Equus, the modern horse, from the Ice Age and Recent

forefoot

THE ORIGIN, USE AND CARE OF HORSES

Ancestry

With the exception of a few minor gaps, the fossil record of horse evolution is remarkably complete. Contemporary members of the horse family all belong to the genus *Equus* and include zebras and donkeys as well as *Equus caballus*, the domesticated horse. The group, as a whole, began with *Hyracotherium* (formerly *Eohippus*), a sleek, terrier-sized mammal, browsing on the leaves of its forest environment some 60 to 50 million years ago. *Hyracotherium* had four toes on the front and three on its hind feet. Its teeth were those of a vegetarian; that is, they were squared off on top for good grinding action, but they were quite small compared to those of modern horses.

This early horse was widely distributed throughout North America and Eurasia. However, *Hyracotherium* became extinct in the Old World, and from then on horse evolution continued solely on the North American continent. All the many different kinds of horses that appeared subsequently in other regions, in Eurasia, Africa and South America, emigrated at different times from North America.

Strangely enough, *Equus* became extinct in North America during the Ice Age, not to return until the coming of the Spanish conquistadors with their domesticated horses.

The modern horse is the culmination of but one of several lines of horse evolution. *Equus* has become adapted to roaming and grazing on the open prairies that replaced many forested areas some 30 million years ago. Its tall legs end in but a single toe, tipped by one large 'overgrown' nail called a hoof. The teeth are elongated and coated with resistant cement suited for the grinding up hard-to-chew grasses. Several of its intermediary ancestors were three-toed but with functional emphasis on the middle digit.

Today there is only one species of wild horse in existence — the Mongolian wild horse (see page 134) — now confined to the Gobi Desert.

There are two main groups of domestic horses today: the northern or cold-blooded group, which was originally bred in central Europe, and the southern or hot-blooded group. Interbreeding has produced a third group, the 'warm-bloodeds'.

Original uses

Hunting and war

One of the earliest representations of a man mounted on horse-back is of an Egyptian, about 2000 B.C. Probably this daring feat occurred among many different peoples, at roughly the same time, but horses were driven before they were ridden to any great extent.

The Assyrians and the Persians hunted with the use of chariots, but a bas relief of around 600 B.C. depicts an Assyrian king on horseback spearing a lion. The great horse expert,

Xenophon, galloped across country after gazelle and wild boar.

Horses have always played an important part in hunting, and hunting has always been considered the sport of royalty. There are numerous examples of this throughout history. Anglo-Saxons resented William the Conqueror's Forest Laws which interfered with their hunting. Richard Coeur de Lion pursued a stag from Sherwood Forest to Yorkshire. Elizabeth I rode to the chase as assiduously as her father, Henry VIII. Today hunting is still a popular sport, although wild boar have been replaced by the fox.

The first English war horses were of stunted pony size and merely conveyed the warriors to battle by chariot. As better horses were bred they and the chariots became weapons of war, fighting equipment well demonstrated by the Celtic Queen Boadicea.

The 'knights of old' were small men, and it is unlikely that their coursers were very big horses. The Saracens rode rings around the Crusaders, who soon acquired the same type of speedy, maneuverable horse. Mass cavalry was not employed in Europe until the 17th century.

Thousands of horses have been involved, and killed, in every war and campaign up to World War II. In World War I there were appalling losses among artillery, draft and pack horses. Although tanks and trench warfare gave no opportunity for any large mounted attack, there were many instances of the cavalry's proverbial courage and dash.

Today military horses are confined to the more peaceful pastimes of the parade ground.

Racing, polo and jousting

Racing was known in Syria and Arabia hundreds of years before Christ. The early Romans and Greeks became expert horsemen, and chariot racing soon became a popular, exciting and dangerous sport.

It was the Romans who introduced horse racing to Britain, although some Germanic tribes had been racing for many centuries. But it was not until the time of James I (1603–25) that public races became established in England. James bred Oriental racehorses at Newmarket and introduced his court to racing. Charles II (1660–85) also encouraged the sport and established regular spring and autumn meetings. Under George I and George II, horse racing was part of the Brit-

Medieval knights kept their coursers for war, but for jousting retained prized, highly trained destriers (*dextrarius*—right) so called because they never swerved inward toward the opposing horse and broke away to the right at the last moment.

8

ish way of life, and in 1753 the Jockey Club was founded.

Persian art depicts colorful riders on rotund Oriental horses, unmistakably playing polo—with curiously modern-looking sticks. The game, portrayed on ancient Persian manuscript illuminations, originated from 'Savlajam', a variety of Tchigan, which was a dangerous mounted form of tennis. Polo came to England, via India, in 1869 and still remains a very popular pastime there. The game was introduced in the United States in 1883.

In Isfahan, more than four centuries ago, the renowned Shah Abbas used to sit on the high, wooden-pillared balcony of the Aali Qapur, to watch polo being played below. This beautiful pavilion, and the original stone goal posts, still remain. But instead of the sandy, hoof-printed space of long ago, the meidan is now flower-filled, with an ornamental pool reflecting the slender spires and blue and gold domes of the centuries old mosques.

In medieval Europe jousting was a popular sport. A joust was single, originally deadly combat between two mounted knights. By the mid-13th century jousting tournaments were organized entertainment, held in specially cleared fields. A l'outrance was jousting to the death; a plaisance was for fun, with points scored for splintering the lance and unhorsing the opponent. It was an execrable foul to strike another's horse.

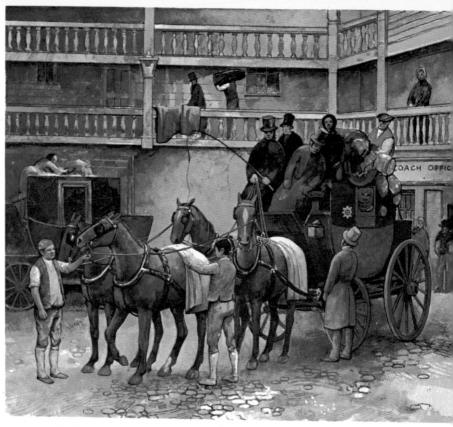

British mail coach (1830)

Transport

Horses were used as pack animals before they were either driven or ridden. The commerce of the Roman Empire depended on pack-trains, as it did throughout Europe in medieval times. In the 1690's a regular pack-horse goods service ran between Exeter and London, England, but by 1830 only peddlers had pack-horses and used them.

The first private coaches were expensive, cumbersome and strictly for the aristocracy. Although they had a luxurious interior the whole structure rested on solid beams and jerked and bounded over the rough roads drawn by four great horses. The nobility were sometimes conveyed in ornamental pole-slung litters, supported fore and aft by shaft horses.

The 17th century brought stagecoaches, but since springs were not invented until the beginning of the 18th century, most people still traveled on horseback.

In Britain until the regular stage and mail coach services of 1786, the mail was carried by horn-blowing, 'spatterdashed' (top-booted) horsemen. They were restricted to a top speed of 7 m.p.h. unlike the relay riders, stationed at approximately 15-mile intervals, of the short-lived (18 months beginning April 1860) Pony Express, who galloped the mails across America.

The departure of the dashing mail coach, with its quality horses, was one of the famous sights of London; but with the arrival of the railroads the coaching era came to an end. However, the urban streets continued to resound with the clatter of horse-drawn vehicles, buses, four-wheeled 'Growlers' and Hansom Cabs, swaying fire-engines dashing by at the gallop and the elegant carriages of the gentry. With the arrival of the automobile, the horse-drawn vehicle gradually disappeared in North America as well as in Europe.

The covered wagons of the Boers and American settlers made possible the opening up of their vast countries. The almost indestructible Concord coaches, built by an American, not only established communications in the undeveloped West, but did the same for South Africa and Australia. Since man first learned to ride, riding horses have provided transport in every part of the world.

The Conestoga wagon was named after the city in Pennsylvania where it was manufactured.

Agriculture and trade

Years ago one could walk beside a ploughman and his team, and watch the horses throwing their weight into their collars as the gleaming, chocolate-colored slices of earth were turned up by the mold-board. Although some ox-ploughing teams were superseded by horses during the Middle Ages, ploughing with horses was not universal until the end of the 19th century or later.

Horses had, however, been involved with agriculture from the earliest days, harrowing behind the plough, harvesting

Milk used to be delivered in this fasion in many rural areas. The milk was measured out to the customers' requirements by means of a ladle.

wheat and taking grain to the mill. The modern harvest lacks the splendor of the teams of Shires or Percherons, Suffolks or Clydesdales, which drew the reaper-and-binder, or hauled the sheaf-piled wagons to the stack yard. Like so many carthorses their era ceased before World War II. Even the ambling gait of the ploughman is no longer a familiar sight. Their curious walk was the result of hours behind a plough with one foot in the furrow and the other on the up-turned earth.

In the last fifty years or so the number of farm horses have become greatly reduced, having been replaced by the tractor and combine harvester. In Europe, and in France in particular, the horse is still a more familiar sight than the tractor although how much longer this will continue is really a

12

matter of speculation.

Cart-horses plodded along the quiet tow-paths of canals pulling long, narrow barges loaded with freight. In towns the butchers' boys used to whip up their cobs as they spanked along delivering the weekend joints; big horses struggled gamely up slippery streets with huge loads of merchandise, and on Sundays hundreds of railroad horses stood patiently in rows in their dimly lit stalls, enjoying a day of rest. The milk-men's horses knew the rounds as well as their masters and always inched up onto the pavement outside houses that might provide a lump of sugar.

Today only a few countries deliver goods by horse transport. It is surprising that in America, the most highly mechanized country in the world, pack-horses are still used to deliver goods to remote places in the Rocky Mountain states.

The circus

Man has trained many of his domestic animals to perform for him. As with all animal training, the fanciful tricks of performing horses are based on the equine leaps and bounds that come naturally to all horses.

In *Love's Labours Lost,* Shakespeare refers to Morocco, a horse that 'danced' before crowded galleries in the courtyard of an inn on Ludgate Hill, but it was not until 1768 that Philip Astley began exhibitions of daring trick-riding.

The circus reached its prime during the 19th century, when famous horsemen thrilled their audiences with the skill and elegance of their trained horses. Perfectly matched, patiently trained liberty horses filled the rings with beautiful equine ballets; hissing naphtha flares reflected the spangled brilliance of lovely ladies leaping through hoops, to land on the broad quarters of imperturbable Rosinbacks.

The European continent has always favored circuses, and the famous Schumanne family have, for generations, excelled in the polish and artistry of their horse presentations, which are extremely popular among audiences of all ages.

Now a form of entertainment that is dying out, the few circuses appearing annually in the United States have become more sophisticated, but some people think of the circus only as a barbarous spectacle of degraded animals, trained by cruelty. Most animals do enjoy 'showing-off'—and circus horses certainly do, as reflected by their fine condition and pride which is obvious to all circus audiences.

With liberty horses 'cracking' whips are the customary indicators, but cues are also given verbally and by the trainer's position. Each horse knows its name and must respond immediately. For looks, intelligence and size, most liberty horses are pure or part Arabian, either geldings or, principally, stallions—debarring mares. Aged between four and seven, with care not to overstrain young horses, the training takes nine to twelve months.

High-school horses may need up to two years schooling, and full routine should not be attempted with horses under five. The animals should be of the best quality, with presence and powerful quarters. Wide, level backs, total imperturbability and a willingness to keep up a smooth, uninterrupted, slow canter are the indispensable attributes of a Rosinback.

Some uses today
Police, advertising and farming
In this nuclear age it is surprising to realize that in cities all over the world police horses still help to control both pedestrians and traffic. There are over 200 horses doing this type of work in New York, and their patience and discipline command enormous respect among the general public.

The well-groomed, quality horses and adept riders add color and attraction to ceremonial occasions, as well as controlling the crowds. Not only are ceremonies and parades always popular as colorful spectacles, but the mounted police have long established their usefulness for patrolling city streets, and they also have the advantage of height for locating the cause of a traffic jam, or the potential trouble spot in a big crowd.

In the past the police horses' size and meticulous training have commanded a healthy, if unwilling respect from rowdies more accustomed to horsepower than horseflesh. It is problematical whether horses should continue to be used for breaking up disturbances, since darts, lighted matches and worse, have been employed against them.

In the African state of Losotho, the entire police force is mounted. The Tehran police horses are all fiery stallions. In Oslo police horses are escorted into retirement by singing school children. The famous Canadian 'Mounties' now keep their horses only for ceremonial occasions like their celebrated Musical Ride.

Horses, other than those used for police and military duties, still play an important part in city life. Some large breweries still keep fine teams of heavy horses with the dual role of impressive advertising and day-to-day deliveries. In Holland horses are used to convey some famous cheeses to city markets.

Even with the highly mechanized farming methods of today, the horse is still useful. Indeed, in some countries it is the tractor that is a rare sight.

The cowboys in the West and the gauchos of South America utilize the horse as their main means of transportation. Australia and New Zealand also have large ranges where the horse has little fear of being superseded in this technical age.

Teams of Shires are becoming quite a familiar sight in London. With high motor taxes, horses are more economical than motorized vehicles.

17

Racing and hunting

The lean body of the thoroughbred, with its extremely long legs, is ideal for racing. Race horses should be kept on a nervous edge in the hope that their pent-up energy will be released to its full advantage on the track. When not racing, or in training, race horses lead a relatively secluded life.

Although race horses do not fold up and take a snooze in the middle of the track, like the temperamental racing camels of the East, strange things occur. The Queen Mother's horse was winning the Grand National when a cramp, or an attempt to jump a shadow, halted it with straddled legs. Another year a broken rein at a crucial moment sent a likely horse careening off course. In 1968 Tim Durant, a 68-year-old American, fell off, remounted and completed the National course. Another National jockey, involved in the historic pile-up of '67, seized his horse and continued — to discover it was the wrong animal! Fred Winter rode the immortal Mandarin to victory in a grueling French steeplechase, minus the bridle — which broke half-way around the course.

Today racing is big business — both in the gambling and the interdependent and highly profitable breeding of bloodstock.

Point-to-point racing is financially the life-blood of most hunts, and until recent years was the province of the authen-

Thoroughbred race horses

A fox hunt

tic hunter, rather than the blood race horses of today.

Hunting on horseback is a sport which is gaining in popularity. It is to be found in parts of the United States, Great Britain, Australia, New Zealand and France. Many of the finest hunters come from the Middle Atlantic states of Pennsylvania, Maryland and Virginia.

A good hunter stands quietly, ignores hounds, horses and 'refusers', and jumps anything from wire to water safely and at any speed. He will go first or last without a fuss, will not pull unduly and has the stamina for two-and-a-half days' hunting a week throughout the season. He is anything from bloodhorse to a native pony and is both rare and extremely expensive.

However, given both a reasonable horse with a good temperament and a sensible owner, good hunters can be made. The quietest horse will 'light up' when hunting. The most experienced horse may kick at hounds on his first day out. 'Little and often' is the young horse's correct introduction to hunting. A tired hunter only reflects his rider's ignorance of good horsemanship.

Polo and gymkhanas

The first public polo game was played in England in 1870. It reached Australia in 1876 and the United States in 1883. The United States and Argentina are among the world's great polo-playing countries today.

The Duke of Edinburgh's enthusiasm for polo matches his skill and he is now considered one of the better British players. Prince Charles is also as keen as his father and is becoming an increasingly experienced player. Their ponies, like most polo ponies since the abolition of the height limit, are usually between 15.1 and 15.3 hands.

Top-class polo ponies are usually Thoroughbred or Argentine x Thoroughbred (the x stands for 'crossed with') costing between $3,000 and $15,000. They normally winter out, come up toward the end of February, and from then onward require skilled schooling, mostly twisting and turning at the canter. They must be fast, obedient, capable of sudden starts, stops and changes in direction, and be responsive to neck-reining.

High-class polo is possibly the most expensive of all sports, but an increasing number of clubs are managing to enjoy moderate polo at reasonable expense. Many pony clubs have sufficient young players to stage an annual tournament. Almost any well-trained horse or pony will play slow polo, provided it has confidence in its rider.

Gymkhana is a popular sport among children in England. Success at gymkhana games depends almost entirely on schooling your pony. Although size is immaterial, small ponies often have the edge on larger ones. Like a polo pony he has got to be quick off the mark and easy to stop. He must be obedient and able to snake in and out of a line of poles without 'going wide' and losing time. In all events your pony should be taught to run beside you on a loose rein without hanging back or pulling; to walk slowly around a bucket while you drop potatoes in it; to carry a straw-filled 'dummy' over the saddle bow without fussing; to stop suddenly while you get off, and remain still for you to mount again; to find nothing distasteful in going up or down steps. This training all comes within the compass of good riding, and however exciting the race, kicking legs and yanking hands only demonstrate the rider's inefficiency.

Gymkhanas are especially popular with British children. They are frequently held in fancy-dress.

Show-jumping
Television helps to maintain the enormous popularity show-jumping enjoys today in Great Britain and much of Europe. Thousands of otherwise 'unhorseminded' people now know and follow the jumping 'stars', and interest themselves in the different styles and successes.

Show-jumping standards are now so high that, even in small shows, the grass-fed pony stands small chance of success. Practically all are stabled, corn-fed and expertly schooled.

Jumpers in the pony class must be 14.2 hands or under, with a half-inch allowance for shoes. Ponies may compete against horses and be ridden by adults in jumping competitions. However, most teenagers graduate to horses when

they reach the age limit. An exception is Marion Coakes, 1967 Ladies World Champion, who still rides the fantastic Thoroughbred pony, Stroller, with which she was so successful as a child.

A good show-jumper is courageous, with a natural aptitude and liking for jumping. Suppleness and obedience are vital, and instilled by schooling. It is believed that excessive jumping, particularly over familiar fences, quickly discourages the horse. Many champion jumpers are scarcely jumped between competitions; however, horses are individualists and require different treatment.

Some horses prefer jumping comparatively slowly, others like speed and enjoy going 'against the clock'; some can attain astonishing heights, although this is seldom favored by horsemen because it over-excites the horses.

Some show-jumpers give of their best at indoor arenas; others appear constricted unless jumping outside. Many small animals win speed contests, because they are handy at cutting corners and changing course quickly.

No show-jumper, however willing and experienced, can excel unless it has confidence in its rider. Riders must learn the best approach and take-off for particular fences, the distance between them, and how to judge and lengthen or shorten their horse's stride. A rider must be 'in tune' with his horse, and fully understand his capabilities and failings.

Trail riding, pony clubs and riding clubs

Trail riding became popular after World War II. It is a splendid means for acquiring a little horse-sense while spending a pleasant day riding through the countryside.

Small horses or ponies are usually best as they are tractable, up-to-weight, sure-footed and suited to slow speeds over rough country. Sometimes each person is assigned a mount to ride and look after, and the treks are organized at different levels of riding competence.

'Combined Events' are another popular, and testing, postwar invention, best described by the French, *'Concours complet d'équitation'*. In both one-day and three-day events the same horse and rider complete three phases, dressage, cross-country and show-jumping. The three-day event also has a grueling steeplechase course, and miles of roads and tracks.

Dressage is a methodical method of schooling for developing horses physically and mentally, Both horse and rider must 'speak the same language'.

The dressage phase in an 'Event' is a set test of varying

Trail riding through the countryside.

The 4-H Club

difficulty, designed to demonstrate both horse's and rider's skills. The cross-country is of several miles, with a number of different so-called 'natural' fences. The show-jumping phase is not competitive, but is a test of both horse and rider, and their ability to negotiate this type of course.

The Pony Club membership exceeds 66,000 and has branches in twenty-two different countries. The membership fee is quite reasonable. Its aim is to encourage 'horse-minded' young people under twenty-one to ride and enjoy all equine sports; to provide riding instruction, to teach the proper care of horses and ponies and to promote the highest ideals of sportsmanship.

Pupils are taught in groups according to ability. Some have the chance to qualify for the Regional and National Rally Teams. Many enjoy fun-filled, hard-working weeks in camp with their ponies. Riding clubs are the natural follow-up to the pony club and combine excellent instruction, competition and enjoyment.

In the United States there are many community riding activities, such as the 4-H Club, where a well-behaved and well-trained horse is most important.

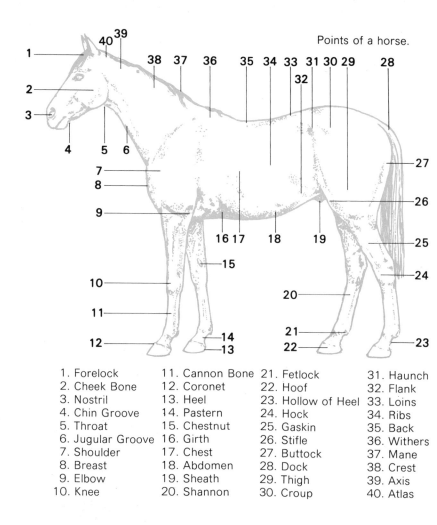

Points of a horse.

1. Forelock	11. Cannon Bone	21. Fetlock	31. Haunch
2. Cheek Bone	12. Coronet	22. Hoof	32. Flank
3. Nostril	13. Heel	23. Hollow of Heel	33. Loins
4. Chin Groove	14. Pastern	24. Hock	34. Ribs
5. Throat	15. Chestnut	25. Gaskin	35. Back
6. Jugular Groove	16. Girth	26. Stifle	36. Withers
7. Shoulder	17. Chest	27. Buttock	37. Mane
8. Breast	18. Abdomen	28. Dock	38. Crest
9. Elbow	19. Sheath	29. Thigh	39. Axis
10. Knee	20. Shannon	30. Croup	40. Atlas

Buying a horse or pony

There should be no thought of buying a horse or pony unless some member of the family knows how to ride and look after it. There should also be somewhere suitable to keep the animal.

Before buying, the beginner should decide what type of horse or pony suits his needs best. In this respect, expert advice will help you to decide what bad points can be ignored, and provide the essential vetting to ensure the soundness of your buy.

Some horses and ponies are allergic to hay and appear

'broken-winded'; others may have 'broken' knees, which may be due to the rider's carelessness, or possibly because the animal is grossly overweight, rather than to a propensity to stumble. These are extreme examples on which only a vet could advise, but if the animal were otherwise intact and reliable, it could be the reasonable buy you are looking for. Sickle hocks are technical malformations, but seldom cause trouble. So unless you want a show animal, there are some minor physical defects that matter less than a good temperament.

Aged, docile ponies that have short legs are suitable for small children. Mercurial types, often with too much 'spirit', are usually unsuitable for beginners—but so are kickalong 'slugs'. Novice adults might consider Fell or Highland ponies and Welsh Cobs. A nicely mannered Cleveland Bay could be right for a heavy man, while 'lightweights' may find a Morgan or Arabian more suitable. Before you decide however, it should be remembered that horses cost more than ponies, both to buy and to keep.

A high price paid for a show horse or pony, is no guarantee of its being an instant winner. So much depends on knowledgeable presentation in the ring, and on the rider's showing or jumping ability. Even an experienced show-jumping pony bought for the novice child is unlikely to be 'in the money' until mutual confidence and understanding have been built up—and that takes time.

Bad points to avoid (a) splayed feet, (b) neck wrongly 'put on', sometimes called a 'ewe-neck'.

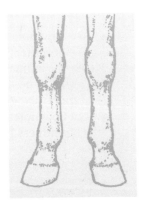

Ponies that just fit their riders are soon outgrown. Larger ponies can, however, be schooled by adults, but riding snobbery sometimes makes adults buy horses when cobs or good-sized ponies might suit their purposes better.

Once the required type of horse or pony is decided upon, the question is where to buy it. The horse magazines and local papers are full of advertisements. These are worth studying as long as they give adequate details in professional language. A 'keen ride' *can* mean 'pulls like a train'; no one inserts 'unsuitable for a novice' unless it is very true.

If you are inexperienced, take a good horseman to try the animal or, better still, arrange for a week's trial. During this time do not expect too much; the animal may find you, and everything else, very strange. But the horse or pony should be easy to catch, quiet in the stable and easy to saddle and bridle. He should stand still when mounted and be amenable to picking up his feet. He must also be undisturbed by traffic, willing to go where asked at any speed and easy to stop. He should jump small obstacles happily, without too much excitement, but unless a potential show-jumper, a refusal at a large, painted fence can be excused.

Horses are sold in sales with a warranty for soundness of wind, limb and eyes—but buying like this is an expert's job. Various country regions hold sales, and there are bargains to be had for those with 'know-how'. No pony, even if it is broken properly, is fit for riding, by physique or temperament, until it is at *least* approaching four—by which time it will be outgrown or unwanted. Friends' horses or ponies can be good buys, but they seldom measure up to their owner's estimation. Even a novice can spot major irregularities. Look the horse over carefully for obvious defects. Pay particular attention to the condition of the eyes and view from the rear how the horse carries himself. His feet should be placed straight ahead of him without any apparant diversion to the side.

A reputable dealer will do his best to meet your requirements, especially if you do not pretend to have knowledge you do not possess. Ask for a reasonable trail, have the animal vetted, and if it is a pony, measured as well.

GENERAL INFORMATION

The horse is one of the most intelligent and versatile of animals, adapting itself readily to any environment and having a memory good enough to find its own way back to its stable, as well as quickly learning commands. A horse can vary in weight from about 300 pounds (a small Shetland pony) to 2,400 pounds (a large draft) and in height from about 3 feet to about 5 feet 8 inches. Height is determined by measuring the amount of hands (one hand equaling 4 inches—the average width of a man's hand) the horse is from the ground to the highest point of the ridge between the shoulder bones. The body of the horse is covered with thick hair, grown every fall and shed every spring.

The horse is a plant-eating animal, eating hay or oats with its lips and grass by biting the blades off with its teeth. Its stomach can hold 18 quarts of food, stored in its intestines. The horse possesses a keen sense of hearing, smell and sight. It eyes, the largest of any land animal, are located on the sides of the head and move independently of each other. Its wide nostrils help it breathe easier when running or working.

The average life span of a horse is about 15 years, and the age is calculated from January 1, regardless of what time of year the animal was born. By the time a young horse is 12 months old, it will have reached about one-half its adult weight. It will continue to grow and develop until it is 5 years old, one year of a man's life equaling 3 years of a horse's.

All male and female horses under one year old are called foals. An adult female is a mare; an adult male, a stallion. A young mare is called a filly; a young male, a colt. Males that will not be used for breeding are called geldings. Breeding usually starts when the mare is between 3 and 4 years old; the young horse being carried for 11 months before being born.

One should not confuse the terms purebred and Thoroughbred. Only about 8 of every 100 horses in the United States are purebred. Thoroughbred refers only to English race horses.

Caring for horses

Crossbred ponies are physically and mentally adapted to living outside all year, but 'blood' ponies and most horses, especially Thoroughbreds and Arabians, do not thrive wintering out and should not be expected to do it. Stabled animals, however, do entail both extra work and expense.

To be fully fit and conditioned, show horses and ponies, and show-jumpers, should be stabled during the season — although an occasional hour night-grazing is beneficial. The 'stars' are normally roughed off for the winter, and then only stabled at night. Full-time hunters summer out and winter in. The general 'all-rounders' can be stabled, according to work and weather.

Most ponies, and some horses, need their summer grazing restricted in order to maintain the proper weight. They can be shut in by day and given a few hours of grazing in the evening with water always available and, if competing, some concentrated feeding such as cubes or oats, etc. Animals that have been clipped can go out for a few hours in suitable winter weather, provided they wear blankets,

Daily grooming is
important to the horse's health.

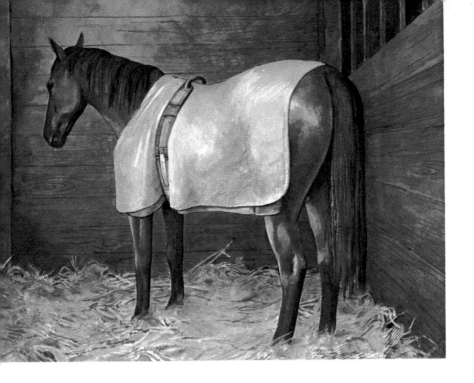

which are adequate covering for most days. This works well if the horse is trace-clipped (the hair removed only from under the neck, sides and belly).

Stabled horses sometimes wear cotton summer sheets. For winter they need a lined blanket. Blankets buckle a-cross the chest and must not strain over the withers.

Stalls should be roomy (measuring at least 10 feet by 10 feet), draft-free and well ventilated. The top halves of the stable doors should remain open, and an extra blanket should be available to provide needed warmth. Drainage, or a soak-away earth floor, and twice-daily 'mucking-out', are necessities. Advice should be sought on deep-litter—which generates sufficient heat to dry off the top layer and with daily removal of droppings, can stay put for months at a time.

Conventional daily renewed bedding, at least a foot thick, is either wheat or barley straw (combine harvest-ing removes the prickles), sawdust or wood shavings (which are good) or peat (more expensive but lasts longer). Oat-straw bedding usually gets eaten.

Horses and ponies should be fed according to individual temperament and the amount of work they do. Stabled animals need three meals a day, at regular intervals, the largest, including most of the hay ration, at night.

The general rule is to feed a horse 1¼ pounds of hay and ½ to ¾ pounds of grain for every 100 pounds it weighs. If the horse does not work hard, it should be fed more hay and less grain. Oats is the standard grain, because it is easy to digest and it contains the elements that a horse needs most. Corn is especially good for providing energy, but it is hard to digest. It should be given in small amounts to the heavier working breeds. Wheat should never exceed 15 percent of the total grain consumption, as it is hard to digest. Bran, linseed meal, cottonseed meal and soy bean oil are rich in protein and should be given in small amounts daily. The best hay is alfalfa, clover and timothy. A horse should also be given one to two ounces of salt each day.

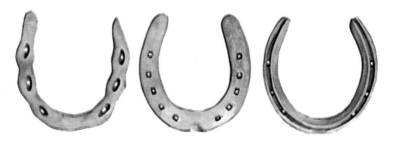

Types of horse shoe. Left to right—Ancient British, Modern flat-cut, Fullered shoe.

In winter all horses need, within reason, as much good hay as they will eat. Hay can be in nets hung high enough not to entangle the feet when empty. Sliced carrots are a welcome addition to an animal's diet.

It is preferable to give water to a horse before it eats. Special care should be taken if a horse is unusually overheated. Give it one swallow at a time until it is satisfied. Horses should be able to graze several hours a day. Grass is nutritious and need be the only food of a non-working horse.

Health and looks also depend on thorough daily grooming and regular exercise, roughly two hours per day, with a day's rest after strenuous hunting or competing. Turning out in a blanket can replace some of the riding exercise.

A hoof pick is used to clean dirt and manure from the horse's feet.

Horses kept outside cannot be as fit as stabled animals, nor capable of the same work. They come of stock used to a wide range of varied and sometimes scanty grazing. Lush, clover leys will make them very fat, and susceptible to Laminitis, a painful foot fever. The ideal is several acres of rough pasture, with an open shed or thick hedges for shelter, and a plentiful supply of fresh water. Fencing should be high and strong, and if of barbed-wire, it *must* be taut, the bottom strand not more than 18 inches from the ground.

Grooming should be done daily. In winter, the grease in the coat keeps out the wet, and profuse manes and tails help maintain warmth. Shaggy coats can hide poor condition, and thin horses and ponies are cold ones. Healthy animals have bright eyes, skins that move easily under the hand, and are willing and interested in their work. Brushing removes dirt and dandruff while helping to keep the coat shiny. Areas touched by the saddle and girth need special attention. The hoof pick removes stones from the feet.

Breeding horses

High-class horse breeding is a science. No horse is perfect, and much rests on deciding which sire or dam, by heredity and conformation, may counteract faults transmitted by the other. There are many experts on bloodlines in this country who will gladly give assistance to the breeder just starting out.

Thoroughbred stallions are often used for improving other breeds, but Arabian sires have even greater potency. Centuries of pure breeding have 'fixed' so many of the best 'warm blood' characteristics, that Arabian blood has an enormous effect—as long as there is some analogy of type. Unsoundness of bone or wind is almost unknown in the desert horse, so that the use of Arabian sires on breeds with such hereditary defects, is especially good. In Europe, particularly, stallions of different breeds are used with the same foundation stock to produce a different type of the same strain, and to be used for different purposes.

Many people with a favorite old mare like to breed from her. This is fine, as long as her conformation is that of a possible brood mare—and she is free of hereditary disease, or of any to which she might transmit a tendency. Accidental unsoundness is immaterial. A suitable stallion may counteract her worst points. Good temperament is essential.

Thoroughbreds are so valuable that the mares normally foal in special 'foaling stalls', under constant, unobtrusive supervision. Many humbler animals, and certainly ponies, usually prefer to make their own arrangements in their own field—if the weather is permissible. Call the vet if foaling seems unduly prolonged.

Foals born in April or later thrive, running out with their dams, but there must be a shed for shelter. At eight weeks the foal may nibble its mother's oats, at six or seven months it may be weaned, but will need a companion—another foal, or good-tempered pony or donkey gelding. An abundance of good food, plus cod-liver oil, lays the foundation for a good horse or pony. Handling from birth and an early introduction to a foal's halter are sensible steps in a foal's education. Unchecked nipping or kick-outs spell trouble when your amusing little foal grows to a hefty yearling, and must therefore be checked from as early an age as possible.

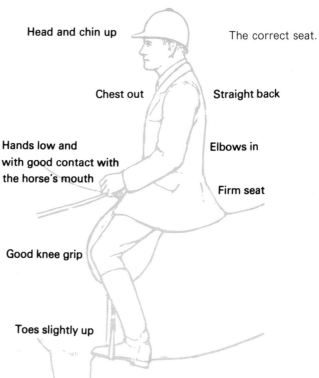

Head and chin up

The correct seat.

Chest out

Straight back

Hands low and
with good contact with
the horse's mouth

Elbows in

Firm seat

Good knee grip

Toes slightly up

Riding

A rider is not necessarily a horseman. He may be adequate at the different paces, remain 'put' over moderate fences and be capable of making quiet horses comply with his wishes. But if he is not 'at one' with his mount, both physically and mentally, if he does not share that indescribable partnership, possible between man and horse, and never feels the mutual confidence that enables them to 'rise to the occasion' together, then he is not a horseman. It takes time, and intuition, but to be a good horseman is to enjoy the ultimate heights of riding.

There are many different methods of riding, each evolved for a different purpose. The jockey, with very short leathers, seat far forward and clear of the saddle, is attuned to the speed of the racehorse. The show-jumper sits deep in order to thrust his horse toward a fence with his seat-bones, and then takes the weight off its loins when airborne. The cowboy's legs are nearly straight, his seat maintained almost entirely by balance—riding 'Western' being the most comfortable position for long hours in the saddle. The Australian Aborigine is a superb stockman and usually rides bareback. The Englishman 'out riding' sits easily, his leathers of a length that is the most comfortable. All these are different examples of the same thing, each rider sharing the lightness, rhythm, balance and understanding that makes them horsemen in harmony with their horses.

The best method of learning to ride is to attend a reputable riding school, where the standard of teaching and condition of the horses is known to be good. Saving a few dollars by going to one of the less reliable schools may result in incorrect or negligible instruction.

Good riding is an art, appearing, to the uninitiated, to obtain the horse's willing cooperation with the minimum effort. Rider and horse must be balanced, the horse's weight distributed beneath you, his head correctly bent to 'accept' the bit. Reins are long enough to give a light contact with his mouth, but short enough for control. Use seat and legs to keep him up to the bit. Slight pressure with right rein and left leg will turn him to the right, with opposite aids for turning left. On circles, use the outside leg further back to prevent the horse's hindquarters

A 'balanced' position

There are various 'seats' in riding, but the General Purpose Seat is the most useful for the ordinary rider. After mastering walking and trotting, the next step is the canter. The rider's seat barely comes away from the saddle, and looking down or leaning forward are incorrect. There must be nothing stiff about the position, with a supple waist, and shoulders and head 'giving' to the rhythm of the canter. With each increase in pace, the reins are shortened slightly to maintain contact.

from swinging out.

The good rider is both relaxed and still. He should sit deep, but light, in the saddle, with thighs and calves providing the grip. Ankles should be unstiffened, feet facing more or less forward, toes up. The lower leg increases speed by slight pressure, but otherwise lies close to the horse's side, without touching. Constant kicking makes the horse unresponsive. Your seat is 'balanced' when you are independent of any support by the reins and of your horse's movement.

Reins are a means of communication and indication through your horse's sensitive mouth (hard mouths come with poor riding). Hands and wrists should be sympathetic, thumbs uppermost and pointing forward, the fingers 'giving' to the horse's mouth like a sponge being squeezed of water. Do not yank your horse to a halt, but keep your hands still with an even pressure on the reins, then push him forward onto his bit with your legs. The schooled horse meets an unyielding surface, 'gives', and slows. Think

Galloping is a pace of four-time, the horse's fastest speed, and should not be attempted by beginners until they have achieved an independent seat, and then only with an obedient horse. At this pace the rider's weight is adjusted forward, and from just above to just below the knee. The seat comes slightly out of the saddle, the body inclining forward in balance with the horse.

of him as a tube of toothpaste, your legs supplying the energy—the paste. You 'push him onto his bit' and apply the cap to the tube—his energy is bottled up between your legs and your hands.

Horses love being talked to, but hate being shouted at. Your voice is an important 'aid', but only raise it when really necessary. Your horse will learn to 'come to call' in the field, and recognize your voice near the stable with a whinny.

You should learn the rudiments of jumping—walking and trotting over very low poles—as you learn to ride. This way the idea of jumping loses any aspect of fear and becomes a natural ingredient of the art of riding.

Finally, remember that a young horse's natural re-action is to swerve away from objects that, to him, appear dangerous. Patience and schooling minimize this tenden-cy, but the good rider is always aware of it. If your horse indicates shying, use of the rein furthest from the feared object, backed up with pressure of both legs, helps to keep him straight. Your voice will reassure and calm him.

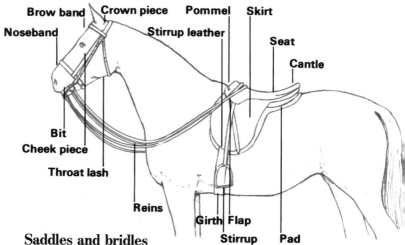

Brow band **Crown piece** **Pommel** **Skirt**
Noseband **Stirrup leather** **Seat**
Cantle
Bit
Cheek piece
Throat lash
Reins
Girth Flap
Stirrup **Pad**

Saddles and bridles

Well-fitting 'tack' add to the comfort and safety of riding. Too big a saddle makes it hard for the rider to sit properly; if too small, knees and thighs may overlap. When the rider is mounted, the saddle bow must not press on the horse's withers; conversely, high-withered horses need cut-back saddles. Seen from the back, there should be an apparent channel, showing that the weight is carried on the big muscles on either side of the horse's spine.

A modern general purpose saddle is an excellent buy. One inch rawhide leathers are comfortable and unbreakable. Stirrups must have ½-inch foot-room and are safest when made of stainless steel. Grass-fat ponies appreciate nylon or string girths; hard, un-oiled leather ones cause girth-galls.

Showing bridles have narrow straps and sewn-in bits. Otherwise, ¾-inch wide is practicable for cheekpieces; billet fastenings make change of bits possible. Brow bands must not constrict the ears—a frequent cause of headshaking. Nylon reins are strong and easy to wash, but can be slippery; laced or plaited leather gives good grip for single reins, leather-covered rubber is also very satisfactory; two reins must be of narrow, plain leather. Cavesson nosebands, loose enough for inserting three fingers, fit an inch below the projecting cheekbones. Dropped nosebands, useful for schooling and pullers, twin with snaffle bits and *must* be fitted correctly—under the bit, in the chin-groove at the back, on the bony part of the nose, well clear of the nostrils in front; just tight enough to keep the mouth closed and exert slight pressure.

Well-schooled horses and ponies carry their heads in the proper position. 'Standing' and 'running' martingales can be used as a temporary measure and, if properly fitted, do not interfere with the horse's jumping.

Snaffle bits should be thick. The jointed variety are simple to use, and are usually effective, but they are relatively severe. Pelhams upset all tenets of good bitting, but most horses and ponies go well in them. Double bridles are excellent for riders who know how to use them. The young horse, well schooled in a vulcanite-mouthed, unjointed snaffle, can be a lovely ride.

Types of bridle. (a) Double bridle (b) Snaffle bit (c) Short cheek Pelham (d) Hackamore—bit-less bridle.

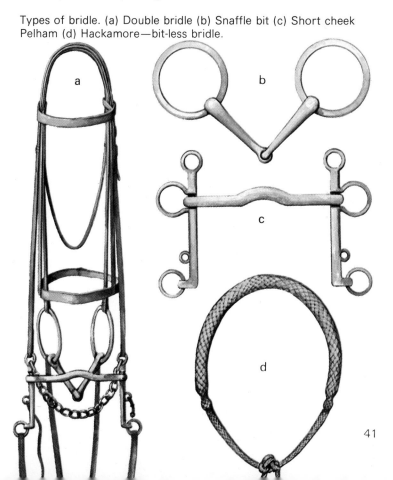

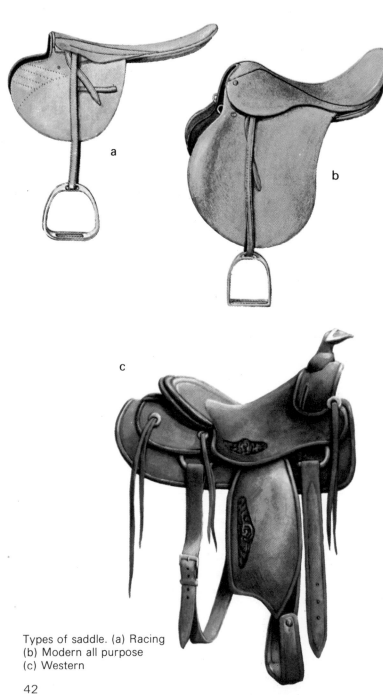

Types of saddle. (a) Racing
(b) Modern all purpose
(c) Western

All bits must be wide enough not to pinch, curb bits lie lower than snaffles, which touch the corners of the lips without wrinkling them. There are innumerable bits of varying severity which are obtainable, but good schooling is always the best method of control.

Leading rein ponies are shown in snaffles; many show ponies and Hacks and Hunters wear double bridles; the majority of polo ponies are played in pelhams with standing martingales; which, once again, contrary to the theory of good bitting, appear to suit all types of horse or pony. A severe bit in soft hands abuses the mouth of an animal much less than a mild bit will in heavy hands.

Many horses and ponies go well in hackamores, which have no bit but act by pressure on the nose. The Bedouin often ride their horses without bits, with a single rope for 'reins'. In 1965, Penelope Morton and Korbous gave a fine display of riding and jumping at the Wembley Horse Show—without a bridle at all. Nsr, a Yemeni stallion, has never worn a bit, but is schooled to high-class dressage, and to show and cross-country jumping.

It is best to remove mud and grease from 'tack' directly after use, and sponge bits. A special lanolin preparation, used at intervals, helps keep leather supple. If hard and neglected, treat with hot, neat's-foot oil. Man-made substitutes for leather bridles are now available and are cleaned simply with a damp rag.

Racing saddles weigh one pound and over; showing saddles have straight-cut panels to display the horse's 'front'; each Metropolitan police horse has its own saddle 'tree'; Bedouin saddles are high, fore and aft; Western saddles were adapted from the Spanish, which came originally from the Arabs; they are very heavy for holding a steer, roped to the front 'horn'; Persian hunting saddles are sometimes comfortably quilted, and the high bow and cantle give wonderful security on mountain slopes; a folded blanket provides the panel for an Army Universal saddle.

The craft of the decorative rawhide and leather braiding that adorns the best saddlery of Mexican vaqueros, Argentine gauchos and cowboys of the American West, came with Cortez and Mendoza—but it is an old Arabian art that arrived in Spain with the Moorish invasion.

HORSES OF THE WORLD

Europe

Austria

The magnificent Lipizzaner stallions that perform the highly controlled and intricate movements of *haute école* in the world-famous Spanish Riding School at Vienna, are bred at the Austrian National Stud at Piber.

Archduke Charles founded the stud at Lipizza in 1580, using Spanish Andalusian-Barbs, a legacy of the Moorish invasion, horses of particular courage and substance, allied to dramatic beauty. Other blood, including Arab, has been introduced, plus a policy of line and selective breeding. Now

The most spectacular movements of
haute école, the *Capriole*

the Piber Lipizzaners are of recognizably different strains, but all share outstanding stamina, intelligence, docility and looks. It takes from three to five years to train a horse to the superlative standards of Vienna and even longer for a man to become qualified as a Bereiter (riding master). Built in the 16th century, the School was originally used for teaching the sons of royal and noble blood. From those days only white stallions have been used. Although the spectacular airs of *haute école* may appear artificial, they have evolved from movements that enhance the impressiveness and safety of the rider, on parade and in battle, such as *capriole,* when the horse leaps high in the air, lashing out with its powerful hind feet.

Powerful draft horses, Pinzgauers and hardy Haflinger ponies do much agricultural and draft work in Austria. The heavier horse, said to have originated in Roman times, now has many ancestors—including Cleveland Bays. Spotted ones make striking circus horses.

Haflingers, sure-footed mountain ponies having some Arab blood, resemble a medieval knight's miniature charger. Pairs are used to pull sleighs up the snowy slopes at St. Moritz, with red harness and silver bells setting off their chestnut coats and flaxen manes and tails.

Lipizzaners have strong bones, short legs and thick, arched necks.

Belgium

As early as the 11th century, Flanders was famous for breeding great horses. Many were exported, and King John imported one hundred stallions to England. These were massive creatures, Roman-nosed and cold-blooded—that is, of the phlegmatic northern type—and the forebears of the Belgian Draft and other cart-breeds of today. They became indispensable as battle horses around A.D. 1300 when fully armored knights needed coursers capable of carrying weight. Later, English crusaders were to find that the lightly armored Infidels, riding Arabian horses, could outpace them, and some of these horses were brought back to England.

Henry VIII rudely likened his Queen, Anne of Cleves, to a Flanders mare, but it was those very qualities of weight and heaviness he derided in his fourth wife, that he most admired in the horses for his fighting men. During his reign, breeding heavy horses was given great impetus, and many weight-carrying animals were imported from Flanders and elsewhere

Belgian Ardennes

in Europe. Belgium, France and Holland, now incorporating Flanders, are still famous for their heavy horses, most of which are linked in ancestry, some breeds being extremely old.

The Belgian Draft horse, up to 17 hands high, with its shapely head, massive quarters and often of the primary colors of roan or sorrel, probably still looks much like those of its type bred during the Middle Ages. This horse is related to an even older breed, the Ardennes, which is thought to trace back to that ancient 'Diluvial Horse' whose remains have been discovered in France. The Belgian Ardennes is a heavier type than its French counterpart, but is lighter and smaller than the Heavy Draft and is popular as a 'middle heavy' agricultural horse. The stallions of both these breeds are used with half-bred mares to produce the Belgian Country Bred, a useful working horse of about 16 hands.

The Belgian warm-bloodhorse has only been evolved comparatively recently from breeds of other countries. There are two types; one for riding, the other a racing trotter. The heavy Belgian horses are much better known and visitors to Ostend on the last Sunday in June may see draft horses, normally used in the fish market, parading in an attractive ceremony, the Blessing of the Sea.

47

The British Isles

In 1310 Edward II imported forty-two Lombardy horses, twelve of which had 'extraordinary strength'. His Archbishop was soon lamenting the cost of so many heavy horses, at three shillings per head, per week, 'enough to keep four or five poor people!'

Crossed with native and imported stock, these horses were the part ancestors of the Great Horse of England, which in turn helped found the Shire. Yet although those famed battle horses could carry a knight in armor, weighing about 450 pounds, their own battle armor will not fit the smallest modern Shire, and judging by the portrayed position of riders' legs, they were not, in fact, the giant horses we imagine. The Shire is the largest draft breed in England today and averages 17 hands in height and weighs a ton or more. Included in the animal's daily working ration, is 15 pounds of bruised oats and 25 pounds of chaffed hay. Two Shires once moved an 18½-ton load over a slippery surface, with the shaft horse under way before its leader was pulling!

Named from the Shires that bred them, these huge, docile

Shire

horses were used extensively for haulage and farm work until replaced by mechanization. Yet even today, some farmers find horses and tractors complementary, and one 1968 horse show had the highest Shire entry for fifteen years. Breweries gain prestige from their heavy horse teams, and it has been established that horse delivery, up to ten miles, costs four shillings per barrel less than by truck. One brewery keeps twenty-eight Shires in the City of London and since 1954 has supplied six grays each year to draw the 4½-ton Lord Mayor's coach for his procession.

Clydesdales are slightly smaller and lighter than Shires and have much white on face and legs. They are said to be descended from native Scottish mares and a Flemish stallion, imported in 1682 by the Duke of Hamilton. Modern Clydesdales date from the middle of the 19th century and became equally popular for town or country haulage.

Unlike Shires and Clydesdales, Suffolk Punches have no 'feather' (long hair above the fetlock). In 1506 they were 'very plain made horses', even 'half horse, half hog'. But if Punches are 'short fat fellows, short legged and barrel bodied', the

Suffolk Punch

modern Suffolk Punch is handsome, too. These, always chestnut, compact, strong and versatile workers, can go long hours without feeding. They trot well, and there is a half-bred Suffolk Punch among the Queen's carriage horses.

Percherons are also clean-legged and have excellent feet — perhaps due to generations working on the 'pavé' of their native France. They arrived in England in 1916, as farm and draft horses. The Queen has a fine pair of dappled gray, half-bred Percherons in the Royal Stalls, but the breed is not common in England today.

Before the roads were fit for wagons, merchandise was carried in panniers on either side of pack-horses, known in the Cleveland district of Yorkshire as 'Chapmans Horses'. These sturdy, short-legged creatures were the part ancestors of the Cleveland Bay and were in great demand for drawing the coaches that first became popular during the reign of Elizabeth I.

In the 18th century, the old Cleveland Bays were improved by two Thoroughbred sires. Later, more Thoroughbred

Anglo-Arab

Cleveland Bays

crossings with some Cleveland mares produced the fine, showy Yorkshire Coach Horses of pre-motoring days.

Owning no cart-horse blood, Cleveland Bays are the only pure breed of general utility horse, equally good for farm work, in harness or under saddle. Crossed with quality mares, the stallions sire first-class heavyweight hunters. The Cleveland Bays in the Royal Stalls have an affinity with the German Oldenburg team purchased for the Queen in 1967. For Oldenburgs, like so many Continental breeds, were originally upgraded with Cleveland Bays. Oldenburgs nearly died out after World War II, and until 1968 were not available outside Germany, only being exported once more from 1968 onward. Now there is a growing demand for Clevelands, quality horses possessing much courage and stamina.

Two thousand years ago the Chinese had high-stepping horses, probably brought in by Spanish traders. In the 16th century, the number of trotting horses a landowner was compelled to keep was in the ratio to his wife's velvet bonnets.

Highland Pony

Modern Hackneys, descendants of the old Norfolk Trotter or
Roadster, plus Dutch Friesian (Harddraver) and Thoroughbred blood, with some Fell and Welsh crossings for the
ponies, were popular for use in most forms of transport before the automobile. But today these spirited horses are too
fiery for any but the most experienced riders to handle in
traffic, and their exaggerated, breath-taking action belongs
principally to the show ring.

A lion challenged an Arabian horse to a sight contest. The
cat distinguished a white pearl in milk—but the horse won by
discerning a black pearl embedded in coal! These purest
bred and most beautiful of all horses have large, low-set eyes as
well as keen sight; concave, gazelle-like profiles, and tapering
muzzles; dark skins and, normally, one less vertebra than
other breeds. Their tails, carried in a plumed arch, are strong
enough to hold aloft a Bedouin rider's wind-tossed cloak. They
have exceptional speed, endurance and frugality; almost every
other breed has an Arabian ancestor, and all registered English

Thoroughbreds trace back to three sires of Arabian blood.

Arabian horses have been known in Britain for centuries; possibly they were introduced by Phoenician traders. They were also imported by James I, Oliver Cromwell and Charles II. Queen Victoria rode a chestnut Arab horse, Hammon, for seventeen years. Today most of our finest Arabians are connected with the famous Crabbet Park and, now dispersed, Hanstead stud. Years of plentiful food and type breeding have produced many larger animals in Britain and countries outside the Middle East than those typical small Arabian horses, now at this time being bred-up from original desert lines at the Royal Stud in Jordan.

Anglo-Arabs have been an established breed in France for many years, and although they combine the virtues of their original parentage—the Thoroughbred's size and scope with the Arabian's qualities—and make admirable hunters, point-to-pointers and eventers, they have no great popularity in England. Lilias, an Anglo-Arab, won a 19th-century Oaks, and in 1966 the unregistered Jonathan was supreme in the Badminton Championship Three Day Event.

English Thoroughbreds, because they have been bred in England for over 250 years—(Thoroughbred from a literal translation of the Arabic *'kehilan'*, meaning 'pure bred all

Thoroughbred

through') originated with native mares, almost certainly of part-Oriental blood, mated to three imported stallions. These were the Byerley Turk (of Arabian blood and possibly purebred) in 1689; the Darley Arabian, about 1700; and the Godolphin Barb (also quite possibly pure Arab), around 1730. Their three close descendants, Eclipse, Matchem and Herod, are the foundation sires of registered English Thoroughbreds, the grays all tracing back to the Alcock Arabian.

These magnificent blood horses are the fastest of all equines. Even today, some show traces of their Arabian ancestry, and the breed also has enormous influence on many other breeds. Thoroughbreds are fine, courageous, sensitive animals, and they need experienced handling and riding.

Some show ponies are fine examples of pure native breeds, but most are part Arab or Thoroughbred. Although showing classes are for different sized ponies (suitable for children of a specified age group), show conditioning and breeding often make these beautiful little animals beyond the capabilities of the average child rider.

Queen Victoria loved the Highland ponies she rode around the Scottish hillsides. They have the ability to 'scramble up over stones, never making a false step'. Locally, and erroneously called Garrons, they are the strongest and largest of the true ponies, hardy and as tough as their natural habitat. They are indispensable to crofters, popular for trekking, and still cart stags, during the deer hunting season, over peat hags

Lundy Pony

New Forest Pony

that defeat even Land-Rovers.

The different types of Highland pony are now merged as one, the best known being the large mainland animals. The breed is very old, but the few remaining ponies on the island of Rhum represent the most ancient strain. There has been some crossing with mainland stock, but the majority of Rhum ponies are still small and sturdy, mostly colored dun or chestnut, many with pale manes and tails.

After World War II, the trekking vogue saved another of our large breeds, the Dales, from extinction. These utility, heavy ponies, are also perfect for the small farmer to use harrowing, in a trap, or to carry him 'sheep looking' over the hills. Originally more or less identical with Fells, the Dales received first a cob cross, to produce trotters for that old northern sport, and then some Clydesdale blood.

At the Royal Windsor Horse Show in 1968, a Fell pony, Balmoral Tartan, was exhibited drawing a French chaise. In 1940, the Queen, then Princess Elizabeth, drove Tartan's grandmother in the same carriage, in a class at the same show. King George V used to breed Fells at Windsor; Queen Elizabeth now has a small stud at Balmoral. Strings of these lusty black ponies used each to tote over 200 pounds of lead in baskets from the mines across the 'jaggin ways' of the Fells to the sea. They covered 200 miles or more in a week and are understandably extremely good walkers.

New Forest ponies are mentioned in the Domesday Book of 1085. These excellent mounts for children and light adults had a mixed heritage until fairly recent breeding within the breed helped to fix the type. Centuries of wet weather and sparse grazing during winter in the forest, have ensured survival of the fittest. The ponies are good 'doers', naturally docile and can be purchased at sales held from August to October. Today there is a growing demand for ponies up to 14.2 hands, despite some contentions that the larger type is untypical, and since it has to be hand-fed, may lose its inherent toughness. New Forest ponies are increasingly popular in other countries. In Denmark there is a flourishing stud, where they breed the larger type.

New Forest mares, Galloways (an extinct Highland strain) and some Arabian blood produced a type of pony that runs, semi-wild, on Lundy Island, off Devon's west coast. Occasionally for sale at Barnstaple Fair, Lundy ponies are hardy, have

Shetland Pony

Exmoor Pony

good temperaments and characteristically thick, protective skins instead of shaggy coats. The island's numerous granite blocks and briar clumps have made them natural jumpers.

Dartmoor ponies have pretty heads and sturdy comformations, plus the kind, stout-hearted character that endears it to child riders. Shetlands, introduced to reduce the size when Dartmoors were popular as pit-ponies, made most of the moorland herds crossbred, but studs throughout the country breed them pure.

Exmoors, slightly larger and preserved pure-bred in their natural habitat, are an ancient breed, not far removed from the Wild Horse. Centuries ago they looked much as they do now — with mealy-colored muzzles, eyelids and underparts, and a characteristic wiry winter coat. Having fended for themselves for generations, Exmoors can be inherently nervous, but experienced handling turns them into excellent riding ponies.

Prince Andrew's fetching, well-behaved little black Shetland, Valkyrie, has now passed down to Prince Edward. Dandy, a white Shetland stallion, inhabits the Royal Jordanian Stables, where he works off his high spirits in rough-and-tumble games with his young Bedouin groom. The elderly,

57

sedate and very hairy Shetland, Persi, wears scarlet Persian trappings and gives pleasure to the Shah's small daughter, Princess Farahnaz. There is a Shetland pony carved on a Pictish monument of A.D. 840. This animal of ancient orgin is particularly hardy, strong and long-lived, and has an average height of 9.3 hands. Although small, Shetlands can carry a man with ease. In their native islands, they often transport peat in 'kelshies', slung either side of the klibber, a wooden saddle. In the United States, selective breeding has produced a more slender pony, better suited to trotting races. Those shown in harness classes somewhat resemble miniature Hackneys, with artificial paces and tails!

My wall-eyed, Irish-bred pony, Twala, has been part of the family for fourteen years. Sturdy enough to carry my husband or myself, he has been ridden by my daughters in everything from Pony Club championships to fancy dress events. He is the perfect family pony, a type of no particular breed but suitable by size and temperament for the youngest and oldest riding members. Twala is imperturbable under all circum-

Connemara Pony

Irish Hunter

stances, including steps, foot-bridges, swimming, picnics and hunting. Like most family ponies, he is worth his weight in gold.

The Irish climate, grass, temperament and 'know-how', has always gone toward producing good horses, including some of the finest steeple-chasers and racehorses in the world. Irish hunters and Irish cobs are types rather than definite breeds, both unfortunately now past their heyday. The cobs, admirably sturdy and versatile, ride-and-drive animals, are particularly hard to find. The hunters are well-made, reliable horses that can really gallop on and jump. A number of international show-jumpers are of this type, including The Rock, one of Italy's best known, successful show-jumpers. They are mostly descendants of Irish Draft mares, with Thoroughbred and Connemara pony blood.

Connemaras have been bred in western Eire for so long that their origins have been lost in time. They have similar forebears to Highland ponies, but with an addition of Arabian, Spanish and Andalusian blood many centuries ago. It is possible that these other breeds were introduced by the rich merchants of Galway City during Ireland's extensive trade with Spain. Another version has it that Andalusian and

Welsh Mountain Pony

Oriental stallions swam ashore from the wrecks of the Spanish Armada. Some Connemara ponies tend to 'amble', that is, move fore and hind feet in pairs together, which could be a legacy from the Irish Hobby of the Middle Ages—a type of ambling pony just under 14 hands, bred from Spanish Jennets. A more recent Arabian cross gave added refinement to this attractive breed, without detracting from their natural hardiness inherited by living on the scanty, rough grazing of the Irish bogs and mountainsides.

Wales possesses some of the most beauiful ponies in the world. There are four types, divided into sections, but all come from the same stock—the Welsh Mountain Pony. All show that special 'look of eagles', the fiery elegance inherited from Arabian forebears. The mountain ponies are the smallest, and come of Celtic stock, probably upgraded by Arabtype animals brought to Britain by the Romans. They have been given added quality by more recent infusions of Arabian blood. These ponies do not exceed 12 hands, but are strong as well as elegant, and sometimes prove too high-couraged and quick in their reactions for novices to ride alone. They make wonderful leading-rein ponies, are very successful in the show ring and go well in harness.

The Section 'B' riding types do not go over 13.2 hands and were founded on mountain ponies that grew too big. They have retained the hardiness and vigor of their origins combined with longer legs and length of stride, and they can jump and gallop like miniature steeple-chasers, besides gaining much success in showing.

The cobby, small hunter, ride-and-drive Section 'C' types, were founded on a cross of the Mountain Pony and Welsh Cob, and they possess the good qualities of both. They make admirable family ponies for those who enjoy driving as well as riding, and are popular for trekking, but they are the least numerous of the 'Welshmen'.

Welsh Cobs are the largest, strongest and perhaps most versatile of all four sections. They are compact animals, usually about 14.2 to 15 hands, with the special advantages of a not-too-large horse that is up to almost any weight, jumps well, and goes in harness. They have great presence and good looks, allied to an equable nature, and the inherited stamina to live out and thrive on relatively little food. All Welsh Cobs should have natural 'fire' and action combining powerful hock leverage with forward floating movement. Since their future now seems to lie with riding, many modern Cobs are being bred without the more exaggerated Hackney-like trot of those exhibited in the old Welsh 'Show-under-Saddle' classes.

Welsh Cob

East Bulgarian

Kladruber

Bulgaria

In 1864 the Turkish overlords established the Kabuik stud to supply horses for their army. In 1878 the country was liberated, and the Bulgars took over the stud and foundation stock, which was predominantly of Arabian strains. More State farms followed, with stallions imported chiefly from Austria, Hungary and Russia.

Today, despite mechanization, many horses are still used on the land and for transport, particularly in the hilly regions. The Union of Physical Culture and Sports encourages all aspects of horsemanship, and Bulgarian horses compete at international races and, with the exception of Tokyo, in the Olympic Equestrian events.

Many modern studs contain sections for English Thoroughbreds as well as for Gidran horses, those Anglo-Arabs of southeast Europe, and the Hungarian Nonius. A policy of selective breeding has produced a first-class crossbred, the East Bulgarian. A compact, good-looking animal, owning both Arab and Thoroughbred blood, it is equally at home working on the land, pulling loads or competing both at dressage and at jumping.

The Plevan is another excellent dual-purpose crossbred, as is the slightly heavier Danubian, a later addition to the list. Heavy horses are bred in some parts of the country, and there is a Bulgarian type of Arab.

Czechoslovakia

In 1916 the last sad duty of the coal-black Kladruber horses from the Royal Stalls in Vienna, was to draw the funeral coach of the Emperor Franz Josef. This Cezchoslovakian breed was named after the Imperial Stud, originally at Kladrub in Bohemia. These splendid animals, all of 17 or 18 hands, used to be driven in teams of six or eight on State occasions.

Kladrubers, only one of several breeds in such a horse-minded country, are used extensively for harness and agricultural work. Close by their stud farm at Slatihany is a fascinating museum devoted to the history of the horse. The stud itself once belonged to a family closely connected with the Grand Pardubice—a grueling steeplechase of international fame, that has been run almost every autumn for the past 150 years.

Denmark

Denmark has always been renowned for horse breeding. The Jutland Draft horse existed in the 12th century and was later imported by England, Germany and France. However, the tractor saw the end of the majority of heavy horses in Denmark, so the Danes set about founding a new sporting horse; animals that would make spirited but good-tempered hacks, hunters and dressage horses, with specimens suitable for all weights. Based on Scandinavian and north German riding-horse types, which mostly trace back to Cleveland Bay stallions, imported during the past 250 years and later improved with Thoroughbreds, any animal of the desired action, conformation and temperament is registered. Many stallions are

Knabstrup

The Fjording is a sturdy, dun colored pony with clipped, upright dun and silver mane, a black stripe down its back and a deserved reputation for sense and good temper.

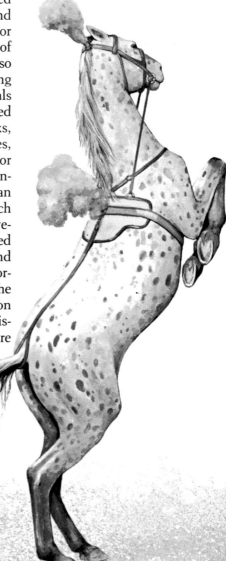

again imported from England, and all potential sires rigorously tested. The subsequent progeny may get a higher register and so on into the stud book.

In 1562, a famous Royal stud near Copenhagen gave its name to Denmark's best-known breed, the Frederiksborg. Founded with mostly Italian Neapolitans and Spanish Andalusians, and thus related to the Lipizzaner, this breed was also treasured for school and parade by medieval knights and cavaliers. Frederiksborgs were nearly finished by World War II, but the breed was revived with German Oldenburgs and East Friesians.

Fredy Knie, the famous Swiss circus trainer, used many Knabstrups in his spectacular acts. Originating at the same stud and akin, if lighter built, to Frederiksborgs, Knabstrups differ chiefly in color. Most Frederiksborgs are chestnut, but all Knabstrups must be spotted, a characteristic founded by Flaebehoppen, a speedy spotted mare of great endurance and Spanish breeding, left in Denmark by Spanish troops during the Napoleonic wars.

These horses have sometimes been bred for spots at the expense of other considerations. Today many so-called Knabstrups bear small resemblance, except for spots, to those which were once the darlings of the European Royal Courts.

65

Finland

Finland evolved two types of the same breed of horse from the same root stock—the country's domestic horse, the local native pony found along the Baltic coast, crossed and bred up with northern 'cold blood' and eastern 'hot blood' animals.

In this way the Finnish Draft and the Finnish Universal combine the best of both worlds. They inherit the quiet, kind, pulling character of the heavy horse, allied to the traits of the innate courage, liveliness and long life of Oriental strains and Thoroughbred blood.

Finnish Universal Trotter

Finnish Draft

The Draft is a medium-weight horse of about 15.2 hands, generally colored bay or brown, and now only rarely black. Today these sturdy horses are gradually disappearing; their usefulness for all kinds of heavy farm work and for draft work deep in the forests has now been superseded by machines.

The Universal, taller and lighter than the Draft, is as its name implies a general purpose animal. In the past it proved indispensable as a transport horse and army remount, but now it too is decreasing in numbers.

Fortunately for the Finnish Universal it can be bred up to make an excellent Trotter, and in this capacity its popularity is assured. Trotting races, evolved from single 'matches' between gentlemen out to prove their horse's superiority on the road, were first popularized in England, reaching a peak in the late 19th century. Legislation and undesirable practices then killed the sport in the United Kingdom, and it is only now struggling to stage a revival. But if trotting disappeared as a recognized sport from the British scene, the enormous success of harness racing in the United States is due, in part, to the blood of imported British trotting stallions in the past. In Europe, as well as in many other countries, this form of racing has a top priority in sport, and in Finland there are thousands of professional and amateur drivers who support the 800 or so Trotting Clubs that flourish throughout the country.

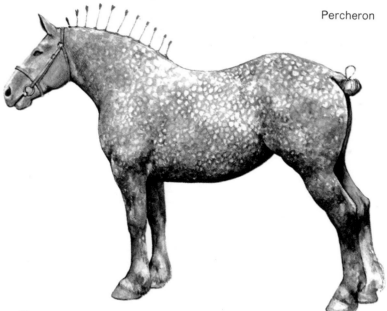

France

Today, France has more heavy breeds than any other country. The excellent Boulonnais, descended from heavy horses crossed with Oriental types ridden by Caesar's legions, and later improved by the Arab and Barb stallions of returned Crusaders, has gone through many changes. Before the railroad era, these horses were used for fast-trotting work, drawing heavy coaches and military equipment. Today, they are massive farm animals that still retain the good looks and conformation implanted by their forebears.

Just as Thoroughbred or Arab blood improves light horses, so that of the Boulonnais betters the 'heavies'. The three types of the popular Breton, the Draft, more cobby Postier and less familiar (Corlay) mountain pony, have all benefited to a great degree in this way.

Julius Caesar approved the Ardennes, a breed thought to be descended from the ancient diluvial horse that once roamed France, and to be an ancestor of the Great Horses of the Middle Ages. Ardennes were sought after as cavalry chargers in the 17th century and as artillery 'wheelers' in World War I. Today, the French version of the Ardennes is a use-

Breton

ful, short-legged, small draft horse, that, given lush feeding, grows into a much heavier animal.

Not long ago, most nurseries contained dappled gray rockinghorses, first modeled on the handsome French Percheron. Introduced into England in 1916, these amenable, active and economical horses rapidly became popular, just as they did in the United States and Canada, but mechanization has inevitably reduced their numbers. Originally a cross of Norman with Oriental horses, hailing from the La Perche region, many Percherons owe their brilliant eyes and delicately cut ears to Napoleon's gray Arab chargers, the stallions Gallipoli and Godolphin. A more recent heavy cross gave added weight, although there is a lighter French type. Both versions are noted for their vigorous trot and ability to pull extremely heavy loads.

Originating in French Hainault, the Trait du Nord that found favor with Caesar for his cavalry, is a heavier but close relative of the Ardennes. Particularly useful in heavy going, these are now farm horses—as are the very similar types, the lighter Auxoise, the taller Seine Inférieure and the Comtois, said to derive from the Bourguignon, mentioned in the 4th century and bred in the 'granary of Burgundy'.

With their heavy heads, thick ears, long bodies and dull dispositions, Poitevine horses appear to have few attractions. But their large feet were useful on the marshy ground where the Dutch were the first to bring them. Crossed with the Baudet de Poitu, the large local jackass, Poitevine mares are invaluable for producing big, first-class mules, some of them over 16 hands.

French Thoroughbreds are very successful race horses. For many years the French invaders have crossed the channel, to capture some of the richest British racing prizes. French Anglo-Arabs, first-class, versatile saddle-horses, have been bred at La Pompadour stud since about 1846, the breed founded by English Thoroughbred stallions with mares of Arab blood. In England, Anglo-Arabs are usually produced by the original cross, but in France they now breed true.

William the Conqueror introduced powerful Norman horses to England. This breed, subsequently crossed with cart-horses, then with Arabs, half-breds and Thoroughbreds,

Poitevine

Camargue Pony

was used with the famous Norfolk Trotter, Young Rattler, to produce French Anglo-Norman horses. Now there is the saddle-horse type, also used to breed up trotters, and a heavy cob.

The Ariège is a tough, energetic Pyrenean pony, less known than the 'wild white horses of the sea'—those small Carmague horses of ancient lineage that roam, in semi-wild herds, among rigorous marshy regions near Arles. Living on pasturage as rough as the wintry weather, they are rounded up by the 'Gardiens', local cowboys and used for herding and working the black fighting bulls of the district. They also carry tourists safely through the dangerous marshes to see flocks of pink flamingoes. An association recently formed to protect these horses has taken a census and plans to register foals from 1969 onward.

Germany

In the winter of 1945, word arrived at the famous Trakehner Stud in East Prussia that the Russians were near. With no time to lose, a nucleus of in-foal mares were harnessed to field-wagons and driven westward, while an old man and two boys set off on foot to herd about thirty stallions in the same direction. The stud and remaining Trakehner and East Prussian horses were eventually taken over by the Poles, who breed them now as Masuren. Those that reached safety provided the core for new, post-war Trakehner studs, now producing a more elegant type, which has much influence on other breeds.

The endurance of Trakehner horses can never be questioned after that desperate nine hundred mile trek. The mares were unshod, and for two-and-a-half months contended with snow, ice and frequent bombing. They mostly remained harnessed through the nights, standing outside ready to move off directly if danger threatened. Fodder was so scarce that the majority of the expected foals were born dead of starvation. Less than one thousand pure-bred horses from East Prussia escaped, but many countries now have Trakehner studs, breeding these courageous animals that excel in riding sports, harness and farm work.

Hanoverians have been bred in northern Germany since English kings of the House of Hanover sent over Thoroughbreds to enhance some of the breed. They also imported

Trakehner

Hanoverian

Hanoverians into their own Royal Stalls as carriage horses.

Prior to World War II Hanoverians were dual-purpose animals, used extensively for farming and in demand as army mounts. After the war, with studs dispersed and breeders dispossessed, a nucleus of registered, and fortunately branded stock was collected. The first priority was to provide animals to replace the almost non-existent tractors and farm horses.

Since 1948, the policy has been to produce quality riding horses, good enough to compete internationally in 'eventing' and on the show ground. Mostly Trakehner stallions, with a few Arabians and Thoroughbreds, have been used with regis-

Dülmen Ponies

tered mares—whose pedigrees state the percentage of alien blood. The stallions are State owned and kept at Celle where, each autumn, they are shown in an attractive public exhibition. At three years old the stallions are rigorously tested before receiving breeding certificates, and they are then sent, in springtime, to farms all over the country.

Some of the Hanoverians' origins are said to lie with two ancient German pony breeds, but there are few, if any, Senner ponies running semi-wild in the Tentoberger Wald nowadays. Hanoverian lineage compares with that of the Dülmen, mentioned in a document of 1316. These small Dülman 'wild horses', all under 13 hands, possess the dorsal black eel stripe of wild horse ancestry, but come in the varied colorings of more domesticated animals. Their home, where they fend entirely for themselves, lies among the moors and forest of the 500 acre preserve belonging to the Dukes of Croy. Be-

tween the annual round-ups, no human feeds or touches
the ponies—which adds to the excitement and is much appreciated by summer visitors. The event is further enhanced
by the picturesque costume of the 'toreros' who conduct it.
Several turbulent hours are spent in catching and branding
the unwanted colts, which are then sold on the spot, mostly
to smallholders and tradesmen, or for eventual riding by children.

The very weighty Rhineland Heavy Draft goes under
several names and types. It has the Ardennes as a common
ancestor with its Belgian counterpart. In the northwest,
Schleswig Heavy Draft horses are vary similar to the Jut-
lands of Denmark. They possess a percentage of Thoroughbred blood which gives them a lively, and willing temperament, combined with heavy, cobby, low-to-the-ground
conformation. At one point, the breed seemed in danger of
dying out, but in the last thirty years it has increased again.

Greece

Greek history and mythology are confusingly interwoven, but both resound with references to horses. Yet no fossils remain to suggest horses were indigenous, and the mountainous terrain is largely unsuitable for horse breeding.

The sea god, Poseidon, created the first horse, and the sun god's chariot was drawn across the sky by a team. Pluto had his black steeds, and Hercules' speedy animal possessed human feet and voice. When Achilles scolded his horse, it promptly foretold his death.

The first horses probably arrived through war and trading. Homer writes of Thracian animals, 'shining like rays of sun at dawn' and 'swifter than the storm'. A war chariot and pair, of about 1600 B.C. is depicted on a tomb at Mycenae, and Xenophon was propounding excellent principles of horsemanship by 300 B.C. His instruction to mount by grasping the mane behind the ears, indicates small horses, as do the famous Parthenon frieze riders—whose feet hang near their sturdy mount's knees. Possibly for this reason the original war chariots were only for transporting the warriors, and the subsequent, ridden war-horses were employed for reconnaissance. By 350 B.C., Phillip of Macedon's cavalry was renowned, and his son Alexander the Great, mastered and owned the celebrated charger, Bucephalus. Chariot racing quickly became the dominating sport. To win was the highest honor, and the victor was then lauded by poets.

Modern Greece is not horse-minded. However, there are Pindos ponies, Oriental in type and around 13 hands, ridden and farm-worked in the hilly Epirus and Thessaly districts; and sturdy, economical Peneia ponies working the land and toting packs in part of the Peloponnese. Used with donkey mares the stallions father good hinnies.

The tiny ponies on the island of Skyros are not unlike Tarpans. They are usually gray or light brown in color and are about 11 hands high when fully grown. Possibly like Shetlands, they owe their lack of inches to centuries of poor pasture. Some are used in other parts of Greece for teaching small children to ride, but the breed, decimated by disease and lack of food was rapidly dying out. Now a British-inspired society is establishing their preservation.

Horses depicted on the Parthenon frieze, in the British Museum.

Gelderland

Holland

In 1662, English horses were described as '. . . (neither) so slovenly as the Flemish . . . nor so earthy as those in the low countries . . . '—an unflattering allusion that might fit the so-called 'Flanders mare' type, but which could be scarcely less true of the proud, picturesque Friesian. A hard-working horse with profuse mane and tail, a high-actioned active trot and a good tempered but sensitive nature, that does '. . . not suffer fools gladly'. The original Friesians were used in war-chariots of early Christian times. Crossed with Andalusians, they then became one of the most popular horses of the Middle Ages, and appear frequently as Knights' coursers in the paintings of the old Dutch masters. In 1644, a Princess of Oldenburg gave the Duke of Newcastle a 'Friesland' horse. Later, they found favor as harness and farm horses, just as they do in any number of places today.

Shortly before World War I, only three Friesian stallions remained, but some imaginative Friesian farmers managed to preserve their excellent horses by rebuilding the breed with careful use of Oldenburgs and the remaining stock. Trotting was popular in Holland long before it became a world-wide sport and exported Friesian (Harddraver) horses helped to found the American and other Trotters.

Many of the decoratively uniformed Dutch Mounted Police accompanying Royal processions at The Hague or Amsterdam, ride Gelderland horses, and the team that pulls Queen Juliana of the Netherlands' coach is likely to be of the same good breed. There have been Gelderland carriage horses in the Royal stalls at Buckingham Palace for many years, although more, lighter built Cleveland Bays are now being used. But the placid temperaments and showy good looks of the Dutch harness horses, ensure that some will always be retained. In their homeland they also do farm work and are able show jumpers.

The Groningen is heavier than the Gelderland, but unfortunately this docile, hard-working breed is dying out.

Friesian

Hungary

Most of the horse breeding is carried on at State-owned studs, one of the best known being at Babolna, established in 1789. Here the celebrated Shagya Arabs are bred, elegant horses of about 15 hands and named after the stallion that founded the breed. Shagya was a pure-bred, desert Arabian that was imported into Hungary and crossed with Oriental but non-pedigree mares. Except that Shagyas do not always have markedly concave profiles, they show all the Arabian characteristics of looks and temperament and are very beautiful. Lipizzaners are extensively bred in Hungary, and there are traces of Babolna Shagya blood in the Swiss Freiberger breed.

Nonius horses are usually dark bay in color, quiet, willing and with good action. They make useful farm and military horses and are particularly valuable for crossing with other breeds. The two types, one more massive and up to 17 hands, the other about 15 hands, are both heavier than other breeds of Hungarian horses.

Nonius

Iceland ponies

Iceland

Horse fighting was once a great sport in Iceland, horseflesh being the staple diet. Today the sturdy, docile Icelandic ponies each year carry a growing number of trekkers safely across the great fields of black basalt that cover most of the island, taking them, sometimes in spectacular sunsets, to view natural wonders such as towering, glinting glaciers, boiling springs, and spouting geysers and fissures.

The ponies are descended from those brought by migrating Norsemen in the 9th century, later crossed with those accompanying settlers from the Western Isles. They are 12 to 13 hands, mostly dun or gray, and adept at finding their way home. There are two types, the draft and the riding pony, which possesses a distinctive, very comfortable trotting amble, known as the *tφlt*. All horses and ponies have an inbuilt homing instinct, but it is particularly strongly developed in Iceland ponies. In fact, at the conclusion of a trek many of these attractive little creatures are loosed to find their own way home, and it is very seldom indeed that a pony does not do so within the expected twenty-four hours.

Italy

King James I, already bored with heavy horses, received a gift of a 'dozen gallant mares with foals, four horses and eleven stallions', all heavy Neapolitan Coursers, which arrived at Greenwich Palace on April 3, 1605. Any disappointment was misplaced, for these noble animals, with their Spanish blood and 'clustering locks', were part of the current war-machine, and of considerable importance in those times. Neapolitans are part-ancestors of the Frederiksborg and Hanoverian and of many heavy breeds.

Horses were used in Italy during the Iron Age. The small, thick-set Venetian horses of 400 B.C., apparently possessed 'flat noses'. The Roman emperor, Caligula, made his friends dine with his favorite horse. Some Popes kept large herds running wild. Pope Gregory III forbade the eating of horse-flesh, but he was later ignored by those monks who prepared a special blessing for the delicacy. Henry VIII imported Mantuan (Lombardy) Chargers, for carrying armored men, or riders

with their wives riding pillion. In Florence, horse races were run through the crowded streets and the sport became widely popular. Today the Palio, a celebrated, exciting horse race, ridden bareback and to very local rules for the past 250 years, takes place twice yearly around the central campo at Siena.

In Italy today, horse breeding is State organized and is one of the few countries where Trotters are revered above Thoroughbred race horses. Both Salerno and Calabrese horses possess Thoroughbred blood and some Salernos still own traces of Neapolitan, but they are types, named after their districts of origin rather than specific breeds. First-class as army and riding horses, many are trained at the two renowned equitation centers, Pinerolo and Tor di Quinto—some specifically for sport like the famous show-jumpers Merano and Posillipo, ridden by the even more famous D'Inzeo brothers.

The much sough after, little draft and pack-horses called Avelignese, are basically the same as Austrian Haflingers.

Norway

The citizens of Oslo are very proud of their mounted police force, smart men and well-groomed horses comprising a unit that has been in existence since 1893; their appearance enhances any public ceremony. The city is a peaceful one, but the mounted force is also very efficient in helping to quell occasional disturbances. The horses are imported from Sweden, because of their size, as this helps to deter an unruly crowd. Most indigenous Norwegian equines are small, belonging to the Baltic or Celtic pony group.

The Vikings were keen horsemen, but they did not confine their activities to riding. Horse fighting was a popular sport, and as with many Scandinavian and Teutonic peoples, the sacrifice of white horses was considered essential for placating the gods. The ponies of those days were on the scene long before the Vikings appeared, and they are believed to have been bred in North Europe some 2000 years B.C. These are the Fjording ponies, hardy, good-tempered animals, and even today, they look much like their forebears of the Ice Age. Many

Döle-Gudbrandsdal

European countries find Fjording ponies indispensable for all kinds of land and farm work.

The usually dark-colored, 13-hands Northlands pony, with its small pricked ears and widely spaced eyes, is very similar to the now extinct breed once found on the Lofoten Islands, but outside Norway few people have heard of it. They are very hardy, frugal living ponies, and to look at, not unlike those in Iceland. From time to time, some southern breeds (warmblood) have been introduced, but as often happens under the rigorous climatic conditions of the North, this has had little effect upon the breed.

A mixture of heavy horses from Denmark, used with some Thoroughbred and Trotter stallions, has produced a strong, sturdy animal of about 15 hands called the Döle-Gudbrandsdal. Mostly black or brown in color, with flowing mane and tail, the horse is not unlike a large Fell pony or a less picturesque version of the Dutch Friesian. Where a larger proportion of Trotter blood is used, the result is the Döle Trotter, a very hard type with the conformation of an active harness horse belonging to much the same category as the Finnish Universal Trotter. All future breeding stallions have to undergo a test, and are proved over a 1,000 meter track in a race lasting three minutes.

Herds of Tarpan roamed wild over east European steppes up to 1870, but those in zoos today may not have truly wild forebears. They are characterized by a brown and mouse dun color with a dorsal stripe, dark mane and tail, and sometimes stripes on forelegs and inner thighs. Their coat may change to white in winter. They average about 13 hands high.

Poland

Poland has long been a land of horses and horsemen. Even today the farmers will crowd into their local town to hear a lecture on horse breeding and the best stallions to use—most of which are owned by the State studs. The subject is taken very seriously because correct breeding not only promises a good working strain, but also ensures a good price.

Local fairs are held in most country districts, and although there are vendors of produce such as cabbages, the chief merchandise is livestock. The majority of the horses change hands either in the spring or after the harvest, but there are always a number of animals for sale at these markets at other times of the year. They are driven in through the night, sometimes from a distance of thirty miles, and plod along through the darkness while their drivers sleep: On arrival at the fairground the horses are put into the shafts facing the carts, where the front end, piled with hay, provides an alfresco manger.

Because of the nature of the countryside, the long distances to be covered and a dearth of good roads, it was, and has remained, a country for light and medium horses.

There is often controversy about the origins of horses, but there is no doubt that the wild Tarpan is the common ancestor of many other breeds in the world. But it is a debatable point whether the present-day Tarpan is a truly wild horse. There

86

were a number of Tarpan herds roaming eastern Europe, the Caucasus and parts of Russia, up to about 1870. The last of these animals, a captive, died seven years later. Because of this, the Polish authorities released into two reserves, a number of peasant-owned ponies which bore irrefutable Tarpan characteristics. The peasants had been catching steppe Tarpans for many years, but whether these tamed animals had then interbred with domestic horses has never been decided. Whatever the truth, there are now herds of 'wild' Tarpans living in some forest regions that have the bulging nostrils, longish ears, dorsal stripes and other features of their truly wild ancestors. Many show the distinctive striped forelegs and change to a white winter coat like other denizens in Arctic conditions.

Konik ponies are close relations of Tarpans, but lay no claim to being a wild breed. They are an inch or so larger, of better conformation, and are both good-natured and live longer. Huzuls, which are little smaller than Koniks, may well be a mountain variety of the same pony. Some are considered more or less pure descendants of the Tarpan, but others, of finer type, have Arab blood. Some of these ponies are now living in England.

The Polish cavalry bears a proud name in the history of war. In 1676 Sobieski, the famous Polish general who became king, defeated an entire Turkish army with only 20,000 cavalry of his own. Between the two World Wars, Poland, probably for financial reasons, did not mechanize her army to any extent, and in the tragic days of 1939, the cavalry was hurled against the invading German tanks. Both men and horses were the best

A contingent of Polish cavalry riding Berberbecks.

trained and most daring in the world, but their brave efforts were inevitably unavailing against the weight of armored machines. The invasion was not stopped, and the Polish cavalry was largely destroyed. Probably many of those horses were Berberbecks, animals bred originally at a German stud early in the 19th century, that had been bought by the Polish government, and bred up with Thoroughbreds to make excellent cavalry horses.

When East Germany was evacuated during World War II, the Poles took over many of the studs and horses that had been left behind. The well-proportioned, riding-cum-draft breed called Masuren are of East Prussian stock. Even today the German 'double elk antler' brand can still be seen on the flanks of a few elderly animals. Masuren stallions are used with Konik or local mares to produce the compact, strong Poznan horses. Mainly used for agriculture, those Poznans with a percentage of Thoroughbred, or jumping Masuren blood, make good all-rounders. Another willing, economical type of work horse is the Sokolsk, a breed built on horses from France, Belgium and England.

Polish Thoroughbreds were originally war horses, founded of Orientals, crossed with local mares. From the beginning of the 19th century these were bred up and improved with imported English Thoroughbreds. The Polish Horse Racing

Society was formed in 1841, and although the racing studs were confined to a few wealthy families, these people saw to it that high standards were maintained by importing only the best mares from Germany, France and England.

In 1508, the high-class Chrestowka stud was founded with principally Arabian horses. A proportion of these were sold to the Turks, who, in turn, sold some of them to England, where they were known as 'Turks' or 'Polands'—a practice that created a lot of confusion in the past, when they were thought to be distinct races of horses. During the Great War, much of the Polish pedigree stock was considered representative of its aristocratic owners and was destroyed on this account. It seems inconceivable in these times that, when the owners of the famous Antoniny and Slavut studs were massacred and their homes razed to the ground, a number of their horses were actually tortured and burned alive.

Fine studs of both Arabians and Thoroughbreds were started again between the two wars, but once more sadly decimated during World War II. One of the most famous Arabian sires of

Polish Arab

Polish Anglo-Arab

all time was bred in 1909 at Volynia. This was Skowrenek, a dazzling white horse with the long curved neck, huge eyes and 'dished' profile that characterizes the best of his breed. The stallion was imported to England, sold to a Mr. Musgrave Clark and eventually seen by Lady Wentworth who owned the renowned Crabbet Park Arabian stud. She was so entranced with the horse's beauty and potential that she did not rest until Skowrenek was installed at Crabbet—where he is said to have founded a new dynasty of Arabian horses.

In the past twenty years, the Poles have begun again and created new Arabian studs. Their horses have always been of world repute, and several American studs are founded on Polish Arabian blood. The Poles keep up their high standards by a policy of strict selection based on races held at Levow. They also have the laudable practice of introducing new blood by importing valuable, true desert-bred Arabian horses from the Middle East.

As in France, Anglo-Arabs are of excellent repute and Poland produces beautiful representatives of the breed. Versatile, elegant riding horses, they also go in harness and are often driven in large, spectacular teams.

Andalusian

Portugal

Horse breeding is on the decline in Portugal, despite the country's two fine breeds of horse, and the native Minho, or Garrano pony. However, visitors to the Algarve can still enjoy driving in carriages which are for hire. The smaller Spanish Sorraia pony, an obvious close relation to the Polish Tarpan, is found in some parts of Portugal, but Minhos make up about three-quarters of the entire equine population. They are thought to be descendants of those horses of long ago that served as models for old Stone Age paintings — which can be seen on the wall of the Cave of Altamira, in Spain.

Minhos also probably helped to found both Alters and Lusitanos. These two breeds, in turn, had some bearing on others of importance in the Middle Ages, such as the old Neapolitan of Italy, or ones still known, like the Frederiksborg and Lipizzaner — though not to the same extent as the famous Spanish Andalusian. An Alter stallion, sent to Brazil more than a hundred years ago, founded the Mangalarga breed. A slight, speedy type of Andalusian is used in the Portuguese bull-rings, where the horses have to twist and turn quickly to avoid experienced bulls that wish to live to fight another day.

Queen Elizabeth II owns a fine Lusitano stallion called Bussaco, given to her by Portuguese President Salazar in 1957. At first, no one was sure what role the chestnut horse should play in the Windsor stalls. He was not then needed for breeding, and stallions are not always suitable as hacks. However, Bussaco is so gentle and willing that he was frequently ridden, sometimes by the Queen herself. He is beautifully schooled, quiet and very responsive to the aids'. Now on loan to a Gloucestershire stud, Bussaco has the unusual privilege for a stallion, of exercising himself alone in a paddock. He is no trouble, but exhibits a harmless, if scarifying display of high spirits, before being caught. Used with quality Anglo-Arab, Thoroughbred and show-pony mares, it is hoped that Bussaco's offspring will inherit their sire's bone, substance and charming temperament.

Lusitano

Andalusian

Sorraia

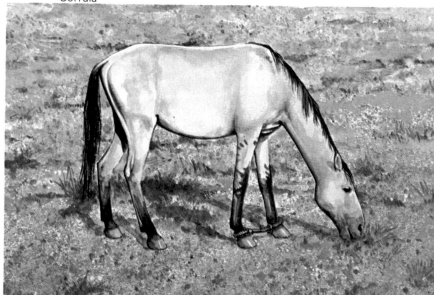

Spain

Horses were in use in Spain as early as 1000 B.C., and Spanish breeds have influenced Continental and American horses.

Barbs and Oriental types, introduced with the Muslim conquest of the 8th century, bred with the characteristically large-headed native stock, and later crossings produced the beautiful and docile Spanish Jennet of the Middle Ages — named more for their ambling pace than as a specific breed.

Many of Richard I's knights rode Spanish destriers. The quality of Spanish horses was also recognized in Edward II's reign. In the 17th century, the Duke of Newcastle considered them 'the gentlemen and princes of their kind'.

The Spanish discoverers of the 15th century were the first to re-introduce horses to the New World since the vast prehistoric herds became extinct. Without these horses, on which the Spaniards relied for transport, the growth of discovery and conquest would have been retarded for centuries.

The Duke of Buckingham, who was sent to negotiate an alliance between Prince Charles (later Charles I) and the Infanta Maria, was bought off with gifts and shiploads of Spanish horses — most of which reached the Duke's friends instead of the Royal stalls.

In 1774, Andalusian horses were described as having 'thick necks with much mane . . . a fiery eye and noble bearing. Horses of pomp and ceremony'. Today they are lighter and speedier, but they retain their distinguished bearing and elegant action. In 1968, a British stallion, Lympne Golden Espanto, of Thoroughbred and champion Hungarian Shagya blood, was shipped to Spain as a gift to the celebrated horseman, Senor Peralta, for use with the Andalusians at his stud near Seville.

Another, less familiar breed, the Carthusian, is an Oriental type, and there are many fine strains of the original type of Arabian horse in the country.

The native pony of Spain is called the Sorraia, but it has not become as domesticated as the native ponies of other countries. It has remained true to the original type and shows a remarkable similarity to Przewalski's horse — with the same characteristic stripes on its legs, a dorsal stripe and pale dun in color, but its conformation more like that of the Tarpan.

Sweden

The Swedes were reputed to have good horses in 500 B.C. Although breeding has been organized for over 300 years and is now government sponsored, there was no suitable Swedish breed to found the original studs.

Through the years, the Swedish warm-blood horse of today has become a composite mixture of East Prussian, particularly the Trakehner, Thoroughbred and Arab horses. Hanoverians, and a few quality Hungarian horses were also introduced to the breed at the beginning of the century. Selective breeding for good temperament, as well as conformation, has produced the Swedish Saddle Horse, a good-looking, keen yet temperate animal, elegant, up to weight and much in demand by the military, mounted police, civilians, for riding in international events and for a growing export trade.

Draft breeds are mostly represented by the Ardennes, first imported in 1837, Clydesdales and the North Swedish, similar to the Norwegian Döle and equally hardy and energetic. The main stud is located at Wagen. North Swedish horses are medium sized with deep bodies, clean legs and of a sound constitution. They are usually dun in color with black points although brown and chestnut is common. They are long-lived, energetic and used in agriculture and forestry.

The North Swedish Trotter is the only cold-blooded trotter in the world. It has also been called the Nord Hestur. They are usually chestnut or brown and about 15 hands high.

Some years ago, excavations in a Gotland cave produced skeletons of a Stone Age pony—the forebears of the Gotland or Russ. These are small attractive ponies of good temperament and of a uniform type produced of late years by selective breeding. They have little 'outside' blood, although a Syrian and an Oriental stallion were introduced about a hundred years ago.

Originally all the ponies ran wild and untended in the forests, as indicated by their other name, Skogsbagge, which means 'small ram dwelling in the woods', but today only a proportion live semi-wild on a moor called Logsta Hed. The rest are domesticated and in demand as children's ponies.

About the beginning of the 19th century, the ponies were exported in large numbers to England, Germany and Belgium, for work in the mines, and the breed was saved only by the efforts of the Gotland Pony Club and interested farmers.

Swedish warm-blood

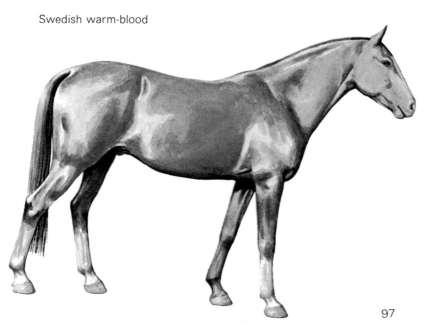

Einsiedlers

Switzerland
Despite the mountains and 'all electric' appearance of the
principal towns, Switzerland is a horse-minded country.
There is no native breed, and since World War II the studs
have been steadily built up, all founded on imported animals.

In 1965 a party set out over the 7,000 feet Panzier Pass, to
ride the route taken by General Suvaroff retreating from the
French during the Napoleonic Wars. Thirty years before, there
were still a few Swiss descendants of the ponies of Icelandic
stock, which the General had bartered for food, but the modern
party rode Icelandic ponies recently re-introduced into
Switzerland. Unlike Suvaroff's decimated forces, they had
neither enemy fire, near starvation, nor winter weather to
contend with, but snow, fog and precipitous going, to test the
famed toughness of ponies that normally live at lower alti-
tudes. All of them took the trek in their stride.

The practical Swiss breed dual-purpose horses of equable
temperaments. Swiss Anglo-Normans, used for both draft
and riding, make good army remounts. The heavier Swiss
Holsteins are also used extensively for farm work. At Aven-
ches, a modern Freiberger is bred, a compact, elegant horse,

based on the old type, with Norman, Postier Breton and Hungarian Shagya crossings. The Einsiedler, a very similar type, is a ride, drive and army horse. Swiss horses and riders are very successful in international equestrian events.

Show-jumping is popular, held in winter on frozen lakes where powdery snow makes an excellent surface. There, too, race-horses, many of Thoroughbred blood, compete in flat and hurdle events, draw light sleighs (instead of sulkies) in trotting contests, or tow ski-shod drivers attached by traces and reins in perilously exciting Ski-Joring races.

The sleigh-horses, with their decorative head plumes and jangling bells, are part of the ski-resort scene. Their winter work is hard, averaging eight hours a day with journeys of up to twelve miles. However, the horses feed well on silage, uncrushed oats and the handful of salt that gives their coat a bloom. In summer, they cart hay.

Freiberger

Yugoslavia

Lipizzaners are usually associated with the Spanish Riding School in Vienna, but the breed originated in the Karst region of north Yugoslavia, where the Archduke Charles established a stud at Lipizza in the 16th century. They are now bred at the Austrian State Stud at Piber, close to the Yugoslav border, and are considered an Austro-Yugoslav breed that is also bred in Hungary.

The stallions that perform '*haute école*' in Vienna are all born black, turning gray and then white as they age, but there are also bay and chestnut Lipizzaners. They mature late but are long lived; they are economical to keep, and are active workers with an inherent obedience. Lipizzaners vary in height from 14 to 16 hands.

In Yugoslavia the many virtues of these horses have been appreciated for a very long time. Centuries before, the Greeks also thought highly of this breed, and on the Parthenon frieze now in the British Museum one is reminded of the Lipizzaner performing 'high school' movements. Although Lipizzaners, like their medieval ancestors, make particularly impressive

Lipizzaners

ceremonial horses, they are also admirable for all kinds of farm work—and appreciated in this role by the small farmers, especially in the north and northwest of the country where

the majority of Lipizzaners are found. Their activity and stamina make horses of this breed especially suitable for harness work. A four-in-hand of gray Lipizzaners would be hard to beat for their good looks and driving potential.

In the Middle Ages, Lipizzaners were another of those breeds, all closely related, which were much prized as parade and battle horses. They have always been popular for carriage and circus work, and they also make excellent riding horses.

The Yugosla Bosnian pony is descended from the Tarpan and shares wild horse characteristics with Polish Huzul and Konik, and Swedish Gotland (Russ) ponies. The modern Bosnian has a certain amount of Arab blood and is a very useful, versatile animal. The Yugoslavs also breed the Hungarian Nonius, and as in most other countries, there are studs of Arabian horses.

Cutting Horse

North America

Canada

As modern as Canada is today, there are many horses. They remain indispensable on the cattle ranches. Canadian rodeos and the Calgary Stampede, in particular, are the mecca of every cowboy, and as entertainment they are famous throughout the world. Trail riding is increasingly popular. Many of the larger hotels such as Jasper Park Lodge in the Jasper National Park, Alberta, employ their own cowboys and horses. They take parties of guests, experienced riders or not, on unforgettable tours through the forests and along the shores of vast lakes, with the splendid peaks of the Rockies towering above. As part of the day's adventure, the party may see glimpses of elk and mule deer and sometimes a bull moose.

In 1964, the Canadian Cutting Horse Association brought a team to Britain to give exhibitions at the leading shows. They also presented Prince Philip with a young Cutting Horse, Max Charge, since trained to polo. The favorite sport of 'Cutting' grew out of ranch work, especially separating individual cattle from the herd. The horse must be very fast, agile and muscular, for executing the fantastically sharp turns performed at speed and, above all, full of 'cow sense' — the keenness and ability to outwit and outmaneuver cattle. Cutting Horses are exceptionally sensitive to the slightest 'neck-rein' or shift of weight. The majority of Canadian cattle horses are pure or part-bred American Quarter Horses, but there are many other American breeds in the country.

In 1873, three troops of fifty men each were formed to administer Saskatchewan and other vast regions, at that time all 'without law, order, or security for life or property . . . .'. These men were the first North West Mounted Police, ultimately the Royal Canadian Mounted Police, who with their horses eventually brought justice and peace to white and red men alike and founded a tradition of integrity and efficiency that is respected everywhere. Today the Mounties are highly mechanized, but they still retain a number of horses for ceremonial occasions and for their famed and spectacular Musical Ride. These police horses, all blacks or browns, are bred from half-bred mares and Thoroughbred sires.

United States

The six bay stallions, with one chestnut and one pinto, plus seven mares (five grays, one bay, one chestnut), with which Hernando Cortés set out to conquer Mexico in 1519, were the first horses to be seen on the mainland of the New World for hundreds of thousands of years. No wonder those handsome, Cuban-born offspring of Old Andalusian jennets—which were descended from ancient Iberian mares much crossed with Barbs and Arabs of the Moorish invasion— at first struck terror into the hearts of Indian braves. Those horses and the ones that followed made possible the subsequent discovery and conquest of the North American continent.

The Indians were quick to recognize the worth of these strange creatures, and they began acquiring as many as possible by barter and thieving. They proved superb horsemen, but used the best stallions for riding and took no care over breeding, so that their horses degenerated into a mixed-bred, called the Cayuse, the Indian pony of today.

Inevitably some of those early horses escaped or were abandoned, and thriving unbelievably well in their new environ-

Palomino

Cayuse Ponies

ment, they spread eventually from Mexico up to the Canadian border, founding huge herds of the 'wild horses' of Western legend. Although some of the grace and size of their Spanish predecessors vanished, these feral Mustangs (Spanish *mestengo*—stranger) acquired exceptional stamina, intelligence and alertness. Many were taken for Indian ponies or for the settler's old-type cow-pony which, bred up with other breeds, has become the range horse of today. The majority of American breeds own traces of Mustang blood, but it was unfortunate for those tough, worthwhile Mustangs that their name became almost synonymous with Cayuse. The remaining herds, by then mostly of mixed heritage, were further decimated toward the end of World War II to provide food for European populations. In 1957, a Registry of twenty-five or thirty Spanish Mustang stallions and mares was formed.

While Mustangs were spreading throughout the West, the

eastern settlers were importing many different breeds from the Old World. Horses that, by selective and crossbreeding and under the different climatic and geographic conditions, also founded the essentially American breeds of today.

Quarter Horses have a lengthy history in America, although only comparatively recently recognized as a breed. The earliest quarter-mile racers, competing over short, rough tracks in Virginia, needed to be tough, fast sprinters, exceptionally quick off the mark. Most of those Quarter Horses were of Mustang/Thoroughbred blood, the majority now descended from Janus, a diminutive Thoroughbred brought from England in the mid-18th century. The modern Quarter Horses are sturdy and deep-bodied, with strongly muscled thighs and quarters. They have a very well-balanced stance and their extremely alert responses allow them to move with speed and grace. They also possess a calm, cooperative temperament. The Quarter Horse has an ideal combination of good looks and speed. His head is short and broad with eyes set far apart. The pointed ears are small. The muzzle is short and the jaw is very well developed. The American Quarter Horse Association was formed in Fort Worth, Texas in 1940 to perpetuate and improve the Quarter Horse breed. Registration of foals in the 1960's exceeded 60,000 a year and is increasing steadily. Some, the finer types, are still raced; all Quarter Horses excel as riding horses for working stock, in all rodeo contests and in the increasingly popular Cutting Horse competitions.

Justin Morgan, foaled in Vermont in the late 18th century, was named after his owner, and is the only man to have a breed called after him. Its antecedents are unknown; some say it was a Quarter Horse. It certainly owned Thoroughbred blood, if not conformation, and type-stamped its progeny so effectively that an admirable breed was established between 1795 and 1821. Morgans were used principally as light harness horses and as harness racers until they were ousted from the tracks by less sturdy, but even faster Trotters. Mechanization nearly finished the breed, but modern Morgans have been developed into first-rate saddle horses; the smaller type is now used as a general utility stock and pleasure horse.

Puritanical early settlers got around their objections to the sinful pastime of ridden racing and indulged their sporting instincts by impromptu matches between driven 'roadsters',

Justin Morgan

a recreation that developed into the immensely popular and highly organized trotting races of today. The modern Standardbred, looking much like a more robust but smaller type of Thoroughbred, includes both Trotters, diagonally gaited, and Pacers, laterally gaited like camels. Originally of mixed heritage, including Thoroughbred, Dutch Harddraver and Norfolk Roadster, these horses were bred until 1871 without a fixed standard, which was then established on racing performance.

One of the earliest needs of the settlers was for an amiable, good-looking horse to carry them quickly about their business. They evolved a type known as the Kentucky Saddle Horse, bred up from imports from England and other countries, which, after 1891, evolved into the American Saddle Horse. Other strains have since been introduced, including Morgan and Standardbred, but Thoroughbred now predominates. The result is the most showy and elegant of animals. Some are three-gaited; others, five. The feet are large and weighted with heavy shoes to achieve the vertically elevated movement of the legs. The tail vertebrae are broken surgically to produce a fixed, poised look once the tail heals.

There is Saddler blood, mixed with that of Morgans and Thoroughbreds, in the veins of one of the newer breeds, the

Quarter Horse

Tennessee Walking Horse

Tennessee Walking Horse, but the foundation sire was Black Allen, a Standardbred Trotter, foaled in 1886. These horses' characteristic, comfortable running-walk, is as much appreciated by pleasure riders today as it was by the original plantation owners who evolved it.

A different gait, sure-footed, if not high-stepping, is produced by the Missouri Fox Trotting Horse, a quality animal, long known in its own region, that travels at between five and ten miles an hour, walking briskly in front while trotting behind, and nodding its head to the rhythm of each step.

The American-bred and -owned Sir Ivor won the English Derby of 1968, emphasizing the quality of the American Thoroughbred, as he stormed past his rivals to the finishing post, with an ease and acceleration not to be forgotten. 'The best horse I've ridden!' was the comment by Lester Piggot, Great Britain's champion jockey. The first Thoroughbred was imported into the New World in 1730. At first mated with Mustang and other mares, the merits of the breed were soon realized and it was gradually upgraded and the alien strains bred out.

Cleveland Bays and Hackneys, Shires, Clydesdales and Suffolk Punches, Welsh, Shetland and Connemara ponies, are all to be found in the United States. All these, in common with Belgian, Dutch, French, Scandinavian and other European breeds, have slowly evolved into Americanized versions of the originals. There are also fine studs of Arabian horses, where the larger animals, even up to 16 hands, are preferred.

A Suffolk Punch of any color other than chestnut would point to crossbreeding, as would a bay Percheron but, despite many theories and some prejudice, the ultimate importance of a horse's coloring lies principally in the eye of the beholder. In America there are several color types, each with its own society, although few, as yet, breed true.

There were spotted horses in China 3,000 years ago, and 'leopard-marked' horses, said to have originated on the Arabian coasts, spread as far as India. In the Arabic version of his vision, Zacharias describes the horses 'which went south all over the world' as 'leopard spotted'. The American Appaloosa orig-

inated its coloring in Spain and was later developed as a war horse by the Nez Perce Indians in the Palouse area of Idaho. Appaloosas have pink skins and silky white coats. The spots are 'embossed' and can be felt, and six or so variations of coat pattern are permissible.

The two-colored Pintos (Spanish *pintado* — painted) were also popular with the Indians for their built-in camouflage. Recognized as a breed since 1963, Pintos are either 'Overo', that is, piebald (black/white), or 'Tobiano', skewbald, includes white with any color except black.

The American Albino Horse Club was formed in 1937. The registered horses are of Oriental type, snow-white and dark-eyed, and the stallions are said to be very prepotent in siring all-white progeny.

The majority of the much prized Greek chariot horses were described as Xanthos — coloring often translated as chestnut or dun, but while many Western ranchers insist that Buckskin (dun) horses are the hardiest, with the most 'cow-sense', they do not 'shine like the sun', as Xanthos horses were said to do. They probably looked far more like the modern golden horses of the West, the Palominos, which come in varying shades of iridescent gold with flaxen or silvery manes and tails. Favored by the Kings of Yemen, beloved of Isabella of Spain, today the Palomino may be a Morgan or Tennessee Walking Horse, a Quarter Horse or Arabian or other breed, but as long as he is Palomino in coloring and a fine example of his type, he is likely to be one of the most beautiful horses in the world.

POA stands for Pony of the Americas, a breed that only celebrated its fifteenth anniversary in 1969. These ponies are between 11.2 and 13.2 hands high and are described as a 'happy medium' between the Quarter Horse and Arabian in miniature, with Appaloosa coloring and disposition.

Mexico
Since 1959, the United States has been importing Galicenos from Mexico, the small horses of about 13.2 hands that are thought to be descended from the Gerrano or Minho ponies from Spain and Portugal, brought into the country by the Spaniards, via Hispaniola. They are proving very popular with

Paso Fino

Native Mexican

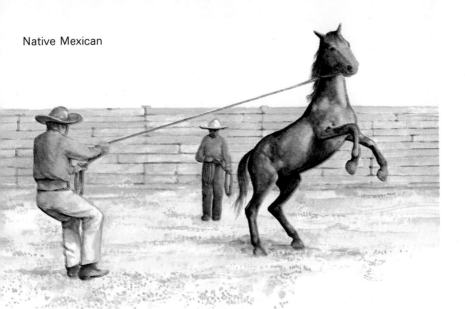

American children as 'in-between' ponies. In Mexico Galicenos are found principally in the coastal areas, where their energetic, natural 'running walk' endears them for all work.

The versatile animal known as the Native Mexican is usually about 15 hands and comes in several different types, based on Arab, Spanish or Criollo. The majority are undoubtedly descendants of those horses left behind in the 16th century by Cortes. They are general saddle horses and indispensable for most forms of activity, work or pleasure.

There have been horses of pure Spanish descent in Puerto Rico for four centuries or more. Yet, although Paso Finos are now being exported to the United States, outside its island home, little is known of this attractive breed.

A process of natural selective breeding has produced tough, hardy little horses of about 14 hands, quiet and gentle by nature, that are capable of the most arduous work across the mountains or in the sugar cane plantations. It is for trail and long distance riding that the Paso Fino really comes into his own. These horses, known locally as 'chongos', all perform what the islanders call 'a four beat single foot' — a singularly comfortable and untiring gait to which the rider can just 'sit down' and enjoy the ride.

South America

The conquistadores and other pioneers brought horses and a common quality of fine horsemanship which was developed even further by the cattle riders of early Spanish colonial days. Because these first Latin American cattle riders were immeasurably tough and superlative horsemen who could ride anything, they were exceptionally fitted for conquering new territory, establishing cattle ranches and providing ready-made, first-class irregular cavalry.

South America is horse country, although breeding is difficult in a few regions because of disease. In 1964 there were around 16 million horses in Brazil alone. Peru is also ideal country for raising fine types, many of which spread into the other republics. Basically, the majority of South American horses are variations of the Criollo—which is a fairly direct descendant of the old Andalusians from Spain, or the similar Portu-

The Brazilian Crioulo is little different from its cousin in Peru,
the Criollo or Costeno and the Morochuco, of more angular
conformation, found in the mountain regions. Both these working
horses are descended from those brought to Brazil by Pizarro in 1532.

guese Alters, and fundamentally that same Mustang which is
so nearly lost to the United States.

Terrain and climate produce their own changes. In the hot,
arid regions of northern Brazil, the original arrivals were of the
Barb type of Andalusian, characteristics they have retained,
allied to the typical 'tucked-up' line of the desert horse. In the
Sao Paulo and other southern regions, the Mangalargo is a
heavier animal, evolved about 100 years ago by re-crossing
with an Andalusian stallion. The breed has been improved
without further introductions of foreign blood, although a Percheron cross was tried—an attempt at getting light- and medium-weight draft animals. In South America, Belgian and
Flemish horses, as well as Percherons, have been imported
from time to time, although heavy horses do not stand up well
to constant heat and flies, and are peculiarly susceptible to
ticks.

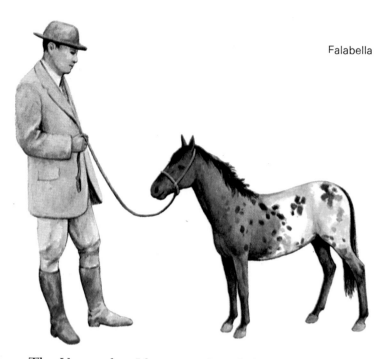

Falabella

The Venezuelan Llaneros ride a lighter, taller type of Criollo with finer limbs, which is named after them—the Llanero, or Prairie Horse. The Chilean type, working in the mountains and usually under great hardship, was noted more for strength than beauty, but has been much improved by careful breeding in the last twenty years or so. It is hoped they retain their sensible ability to grow profuse manes and tails as protection against the flies.

Mancha and Gato were two Argentine Criollos who demonstrated just what a wonderful breed this is. In 1933, Professor Tschiffely obtained two horses from a Patagonian Indian chief, and rode and led them, in turn, over the 10,000 miles from Buenos Aires to Washington. They traveled over mountain ranges, across deserts and through rivers. They endured extremes of heat and cold and ate anything from rotten hay to the leaves of the Pindo palm. Neither horse was ever sick and both lived to a ripe old age, proving beyond doubt that the Criollo is a very strong horse.

Argentine polo ponies, usually Criollo crossed with Thoroughbred, are always in demand in many countries.

Prince Philip owns several, and Prince Charles acquired two in 1968.

About forty years ago a new breed was established in the Buenos Aires province of Falabellas, now a stud of miniature horses all under 7 hands, of various colors including spots, and said to be hardy, intelligent and docile. They began with a very small Thoroughbred, followed by successive small-size breeding with an occasional Shetland cross to help.

South America is indeed a land of horses. In Brazil they say, 'God first made man. He thought better of it and made woman. When He got time He made the horse, which has the courage and spirit of man and the grace and beauty of woman.'

Llanero

Asia
India
Prehistoric equine remains have been found in the Siwalik Hills, and there have been records of horses in India since about 1500 B.C. However, the majority of the country-bred ponies, though varying from district to district, are of similar Mongolian descent, crossed at some time or another with foreign, often Arabian, imports.

Bhutia ponies, bred in Nepal and other regions of the Himalayas, are usually gray and about 13.3 hands. Those called Spiti, bred in the very mountainous Kangra district, near the central spine of the Himalayas, are smaller. They are thick-set, little ponies, with hard, round feet, intelligent heads and remarkably pricked ears, and are said to be both tireless and indestructible—as long as they remain in the Himalayas. Bred almost exclusively by the high-class Hindu tribe, Kanyat, Spitis, like Pegu ponies, can carry heavy loads.

Both India and Iran claim to have originated polo. A 7th-century manuscript describes how the Maharajah of Manipur introduced the game, the players riding sturdy, Mongolian-Arab Manipur ponies. The small Burmese (Shan) hill pony is very similar, although the larger type is strong but slow.

High above a lake in Jamnagar, the capital of Kathiawar, a huge, gold-leaf covered equestrian statue glints in the fierce Indian sun. The rider is an imaginary likeness of Jam Shri Rawalji, founder of the capital, and Nawangar dynasty, in 1535. The horse, intelligent, proud, with the breed's distinguishing ears so close-pricked that only a rupee can pass between, is a replica of Uchaiswa, the Maharajah's favorite Kathiawari stallion of 400 years ago. This was possible because Ashwani Kumar acted as model—one of the long line of this illustrious family of Kathiawari stallions, each picked in turn for breeding for their exact similarity to the original. Ashwani even spent two years in Paris, modeling in the sculptor's studio—his behavior so impeccable that it refuted the suggestion that Kathiawaris are of uncertain temper.

Some say the breed is also descended from Alexander's Grecian horses, others that it originated with a ship-wrecked load of Arabians which swam ashore to mix with country-bred mares in the region

Kathiawari

Iran

Although a centuries old crossroads for the world trade routes to India and China, Persia remained an almost medieval land of mystery until relatively recent times. Now, owing to the present Shah and his father, Iran is modernizing at fantastic speed. Yet despite the motorized traffic loading the wide boulevards of Tehran, the air-conditioned buses and laden trucks thundering along miles of metaled roads and the growing network of railroads and expanding internal air service, it will be many years before horses and donkeys become pleasures, rather than necessities in this vast land. Agriculture yearly becomes more mechanized, yet in many parts, tractors are still a rarity, and where mud walls, for irrigation, enclose small cultivated tracts, machines remain impracticable.

Some of the many nomadic tribes are being settled. Yet even in the desert, southeast of the Caspian Sea, where the once traditionally horse-raising tribe of Turkoman are now mostly prosperous; mechanically minded farmers, droves of semi-wild mares still roam the sandhills close by the Russian border. Prized stallions, swathed in seven, time-honored layers of felt,

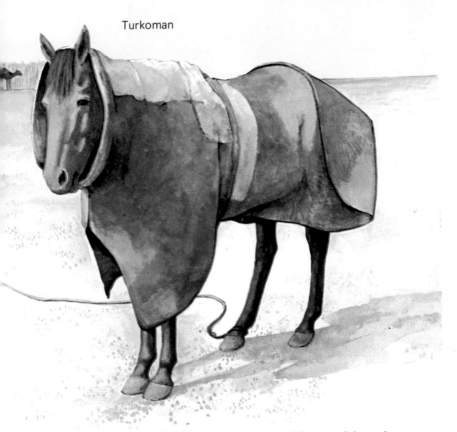

Turkoman

remain tethered beside the concrete, or old-time felt-and-osier 'beehive' homes of their owners. In Turkoman towns, carts rattle to and fro, drawn by the slim desert horses, harnessed with H-shaped wooden collars, their drivers wearing distinguishing black lambskin Turkoman hats.

The original Turkoman horses probably looked much like Przewalski's primitive horses from the Gobi desert, but having been crossed for centuries with Oriental breeds, they are now tall, good-looking animals with the greyhound build of the desert bred, and with a reasonable claim to be the ancestors of the Arab horse. The finest strain, the often uniquely golden-colored Akhal Teke, was chosen for the bodyguards of caliphs of old because of their qualities of exceptional speed and endurance.

Because frontiers are only man-made, at least half of one Turkoman tribe still lives in Russia, and the Russian Akhal Tekes are identical.

Twice a year, the Turkoman ride in through a haze of desert dust for their vivid, colorful race-meetings. The jockeys, usually the lightest members of the family, may be only seven years old, and the horses, unshod as always, compete in events of up to eight miles.

Nowadays, the Turkoman transport their horses by truck to the more sophisticated racing at Tehran. Under a brilliant sun and cloudless sky, against the backcloth of snow-capped peaks of the Elburz range, I watched a seventy-two-year-old jockey ride two Turkoman horses to victory in the presence of the Shah and Empress. Local American and European children raced in honor of the young Crown Prince's birthday, some of them riding little stallions, not unlike miniature Arabians, with characteristic shortened lower jaws and exemplary temperament. They come from a small area between the Elburz and the shores of the Caspian, where they are used mostly for speedy carting in and around the bazaars. They are known locally as Mouleki or Pouseki ponies. Mrs. Firouz, who is trying to preserve them, calls them 'Caspian Ponies', and finds they breed true to type and make wonderful children's ponies.

Twenty-four of the Shah's favorite stallions are housed in one long building at the Royal Stud at Faharabad, outside Tehran. Some of these beautiful animals are gifts, like the Arabian horse presented by ex-King Ibn Saud; the Arab-like Jaf, a Persian and Turkish breed from Kurdistan, presented by the late Turkish President; an English Thoroughbred sent long ago by the President of Pakistan. Tahmiahn, the Shah's splendid pleasure horse, and Azar, a regal animal kept for ceremonial occasions, are half-brothers, both Anglo-Persians. The Thoroughbred cross adds height and even more presence to Persian Arabs, horses of an ancient, fiery and elegant breed, believed by some to be older than the desert Arabian of Jordan, which are taller animals that lack the characteristic 'dished' profile. Koshro, another royal favorite, is a Bajalan Arab, used for mountain hunting, that well satisfies the Shah's love of speed and spirit.

All Persian horses are of Oriental type, but many are crossbred. The Empress rides a fine Turkoman stallion, Shabro, and

Caspian Ponies

Darashouli

many of the royal horses are pure or half-bred Turkomans. Despite their desert breeding, they, and the kindred Tchenarani, soon become excellent mountain horses.

The Darashoul(r)i or Shirazi, are bred in the state of Fars in southern Iran. They too make excellent mountain horses, as I discovered the day we rode for six hours among rock-strewn foothills and along narrow trails, often at seven thousand feet, worn by innumerable moufflon (Asiatic wild sheep), that inhabit the Elburz range. I was riding Shabrang, a coal-black Darashouli stallion with plumed tail and generous eyes, who marched sure-footedly and as though on springs, up and down impossibly precipitous slopes, his scimitar ears tight pricked, his neck superbly arched. Only when my husband decided on an unannounced canter up a boulder scattered valley, did Shabrang lose his equanimity and strive to prove what I suspected—that he is the fifth fastest horse in the Royal Stud! As we rode down the mountains to the foothills that lead eventually to Farahabad, the sky took fire, slashed crimson and magenta, orange and saffron with the dying flames of sunset—and a line of shadow horsemen moved step by step with us down a nearby mountainside.

Japan

Japanese mythology has many references to supernatural horses. In one instance a stallion named Ikezuki has become a legend. Ikezuki was born about 1177 and as a young colt taught itself to swim. Later, while on the way to a fair, it escaped by swimming a river. Its owner eventually caught up with it at the fair but was unable to sell his high-spirited horse. After many such exploits Ikezuki was eventually bought by Yoritomo, a great warrior and victor of the Battle of Dannoura in 1185.

Today many Japanese horses are entirely, or partly, of Western extraction, but often domestically bred. Early in 1968 the Japanese equestrian team purchased European horses for competing in the Olympics in Mexico. Racing and trotting are popular, and in winter horse skiing races are held at the Sappire Race Track. Japan's indigenous breed, the Hokaido pony, belongs to the Mongolian group and is very like the Chinese Pony type. They are small, tough, very sure-footed and thrive on the scantiest feeding.

Until 1874, the mounted police force of Tokyo was represented by a few officers who rode native bred Hokaido ponies. These tough little animals descended from the Mongolian Wild horse are very like that fast, hardy type, the Chinese Pony.

Jordan and the Middle East

In the summer of 1967, the uneasy, never ratified truce between Jordan and Israel ended with the second Arab-Israeli War, and the Israelis occupied the entire west bank of the Jordan, including Jericho.

East of the river and not far from that ancient town, lies Shuna, where, since about 1961 King Hussein's Royal horsemaster has been breeding up the fast disappearing, centuries old lines of desert Arabian horses. On the night in 1967 it became apparent that Israeli forces were close at hand, Rahdi, the Bedouin stud groom, was in charge at Shuna. Quickly he decided what to do. Mustering the other grooms, all Bedouins who would rather die than abandon their horses, Rahdi ordered each man to saddle up a stallion or mare for himself and, where feasible, to lead another. The remainder of the sixty or so horses and young stock were herded between them, and they set out to ride the forty-odd miles to Amman. They went across country, riding up through the mountains by way of precipitous slopes and boulder strewn wadis. The beautiful,

Evacuation of the Royal Stud.

deer-like little horses climbed like cats, with as much confidence, as though the hot sun was warming their backs and they were carrying Princess Muna and her friends on one of those gay outings that were common before the war. Soon after dawn, they came to the big city of Amman straggling up and around the seven hills on which it was built, and Rahdi led his party to Hummar, on the outskirts, where the King and Princess Muna live in a modern, but upretentious villa. Here the horses were housed in recently completed stables. Visitors to Jordan may come to see them, living in dazzling white buildings of graceful Moorish or Spanish design, a fitting setting for horses of such beauty.

Mohammed taught that, 'Every grain of barley given to a horse is entered by God in the Register of Good Works', and his conquests were made possible by the horses his warriors rode. There are many theories about the origins of the Arabian horse. That it is unique among equines is certain, and since

all the earliest movements of horses appear to have been from the north, from Central Asia rather than the other way around, the Persian claim for theirs being the older breed and the Akhal Teke part-ancestor to the Arab horse, could be correct. However, in truth, there is little proof to show either way. Until the Assyrian era, about 745 to 727 B.C., no Arabians were pictured with horses, they were always riding camels. The horse pedigree records date from the 6th century A.D.

The true Arabian desert horse has remained *'asil'*, pure bred, partly because of the Arab's rigid ideas on purity of line, partly due to inbreeding, in a relatively small area, of a comparatively small stock of highly prized animals—that were further culled by natural and human selection for the qualities of intellingence, endurance, alertness and speed, all of which were necessary for survival.

The majority of Arabian horses are *kudsh,* or impure, a term applied to either Arabians of faulty lines or to all horses except pure Arabians. Pedigrees are only kept through the mares, which are valued more for pedigree than for conformation; the opposite being true for the males. The sire of an 'asil' foal, however, must himself be 'asil'. The desert Arabs regard purity of line so rigidly that if a mare has once been mated with a 'kudsh' stallion, all future foals are considered 'kudsh' regardless of the sire.

Tradition has it that there are five strains of 'asil' Arabians, known as *el khamsa* (the five), but authorities disagree on what strains are included. About twenty strains of 'asil' are currently recognized, the most widespread being the Kuhaylan.

From the earliest times, Arabian horses, famed for these qualities, were exported to many countries. Of later years, the Bedouin's increasing poverty and the few pounds obtainable for a foal, however bred, have sometimes tempted the tribes not to be too choosy with selective breeding. By 1961, horses of the pure, old blood lines were getting dangerously scarce in Jordan, and King Hussein asked Santiago Lopez to become Royal Horsemaster and try to remedy the situation.

It proved a fascinating, worthwhile work of love. Sometimes a horse arrives at the stud as a gift for the King, and patient research eventually substantiates the owner's claims for its ancestry; sometimes word arrives of a beautiful stallion of a famous blood line, in the black, goats' hair tents of a sheikh miles away in the desert; or there is the exciting discovery of a mare of the purest breeding among the local police horses or drawing a Bedouin plough. Gradually a nucleus of 'asil' horses was collected, a few of the older mares, now mostly dead or retired, having once belonged to King Abdullah, the present king's grandfather. Skillful breeding has produced stock of indisputable ancestry and beauty, many of the younger animals fathered by Al Baheer, a magnificently bred old stallion that was only discovered a few years ago. Some of the young stock is sold abroad to help enrich the sorely strained Jordanian economy, but numbers of animals, including the lovely Kerima, are retained to build up the stud. Vast sums have been offered for this mare, considered the epitome of Arabian equine beauty, but she is beyond price. Many of the horses are now registered with the British Arab Horse Society, and no animal ever leaves the Royal Stud without the written guarantee that its pedigree is exactly as stated.

The Bedouin cannot afford to 'do' their foals well, and

cow-hocks are common because of this and too-young riding, but although the Royal horses are well fed and without this defect, they seldom make more that 15 hands, nor attain the dimensions of the large type Arabians. Nor would the true desert horse thrive, or be able to cope with its exacting environment, if it did so.

Horses are valuable in the Lebanon and Beirut, and many are part or true Thoroughbreds, or Anglo-Arab types, but there are 'asil' horses too, as there are in Iraq. Sometimes a horse shows all the Arabian characteristics, and in fact traces back many years to an Iraqi stallion, Ahsuri—a Thoroughbred that was disqualified in Beirut as a non-Arabian, before being taken to Iraq and crossed with pure Arabian mares.

The horses used by the Jordanian Royal Guard, chiefly for ceremonial duties, and those of the patrols of mounted police that keep law and order in some villages and parts of the desert, are mostly country-bred Arabian horses, if not of the purest breeding. So too are the majority of the Bedouin horses today, wiry, willing little animals, that are fast, well up-to-weight, and of exceptional endurance and hardiness.

The Jordanian Guard

Mongolia

For centuries the Mongolians looked to their horses, the Mongolian pony, for friendship and food, as objects of worship, weapons for war, and for drink in the form of *kumys,* mares' fermented milk. Today, Mongolia's emblem is a horseman galloping into the rising sun, and despite changes since the country became a republic in 1924, horses remain an integral part of everyday existence. Collective farms, where horses, as well as other domestic animals, are bred extensively, have removed much of the need for a nomadic life. But there are still numbers of Mongolians who, like their ancestors for centuries before them, live by herding huge droves of sheep, goats, cattle and horses, pitching and striking their traditional felt and wooden *yurtas* as they move along the grazing trails.

Horses are still largely used both in harness and for haulage,

and a large percentage of the population remain superb horsemen. A Mongolian 'cowboy' rates it as part of the day's work to capture specified animals from a troop of stampeding mares and stallions, using a lasso, a leather loop on the end of a long bamboo pole, which he wields from his own pony.

Not many years ago, a Mongolian set off to ride home across rough and hilly countryside. He set off at sunrise and arrived at sunset, the distance being more than 100 miles. Mongolian ponies vary according to district and breeding, and in this case it was an 'Iron Hoofed' pony, from Keshitang Banner in eastern Inner Mongolia. Hill-bred ponies of about 13.1 hands are well able to withstand frost and flourish on the poorest food. They are fast, enduring, have an ability to jump, and possess particularly round, hard hooves that, unshod, are capable of handling the roughest going.

In 1879 Colonel Przewalski discovered some of these truly wild horses still living on the border of China and Outer Mongolia, in a small area of the Gobi Desert. With discovery, their numbers were reduced until, from being the rarest animal in the world, Przewalski's horse was once more thought to be extinct—except for a few small herds kept in some European zoos. Then, in 1966, a stallion and seven mares were sighted near the Chinese border. Even those supposedly true

Przewalski's Wild Horse

wild horses may have crossed at some time with feral horses that roam the region, and since they galloped into Communist China nothing further is known of them.

Mongolian emperors were raising ponies in the Shangtu river region three hundred years ago. Today the Shangtu pony is noted for its speed. Ushen ponies have been developed in, and have adapted to, the desert area where they live. They are small, with short legs and broad, sand-withstanding hooves, and have an innate ability to thrive on little food and drink.

In the east of Inner Mongolia, good type Sanho ponies have been improved and bred-up into excellent saddle and draft animals, with the use of Russian Transbaikal, Arab and Thoroughbred blood.

Chinese Pony

China and Korea
Horses are said to have been introduced into China nearly 4000 years B.C. There are very ancient records of a breed, peculiar to one district, that used to sweat blood — an odd characteristic also attributed to old time Spanish Andalusians and to the occasional Arabian horse. The well-known, so-called Chinese Pony, which is also found in Korea and other adjacent lands, is the same type as the Mongolian Pony. Many animals are exported from Mongolia to China for use in racing and polo; they are known as Griffins. Although these ponies are usually only 12.2 to 13 hands, they are very fast, and over short distances they are said to be speedier than the Arabian, and hence flat-racing is a popular sport in China.

The strong, often dun-colored ponies of Tibet are descendants of domesticated Mongolian and Chinese ponies. Wealthy Tibetans, including the Dalai Lhama, used to own small studs — which are almost certainly dispersed by now.

Russia

The State Research Institute of Horse Breeding, formed in 1930, began with a ten-year investigation of all Russian breeds, plus an assessment of the effect of imported horses on Russian ones.

The original Don, the Russian Steppe Horse, was essentially the same as the Mongolian Pony. It was developed by Cossacks settled over the Don River, in need of good saddle horses for their frontier skirmishes with nomadic tribes, and later improved further with Persian and Karabakh blood. The great stamina, weather resistance and weight-carrying ability of Don horses, were exploited fully during the Napoleonic Wars and other campaigns, including the Cossack's unparalleled cavalry exploit of marching to Paris and back. Modern Dons are hard, enduring animals of about 15.2 hands that have been further bred-up with Orlovs and Thoroughbreds. Soviet horses are usually quiet to ride and very versatile, although some buyers can underestimate the immaturity of three and four year olds.

Queen Elizabeth was presented with the Karabakh horse, Zaman, and often rode the little stallion before he was loaned to a stud near Salisbury. These alert, fine-coated and often fiery little horses are frequently bred for racing. Like Zaman, many are of the metallic golden color unique to this and the Akhal Teke breed.

Budjonnys, averaging 16 hands and comparatively heavy, are liked as hunters for their safe, clean jumping. They were evolved about thirty years ago by Marshal Budjonny, at his army stud at Rostov, and because the Marshal required his troops to be distinctive, the bays and blacks were bred out, until practically all Budjonnys were chestnut.

Sturdy native Kirghiz were crossed with Dons and Thoroughbreds to produce the most distinctively saddle-horse type of the Russian mountain breeds. Like the Lokai of Central

Asia, the Kirghiz came of Mongolian stock and possesses great stamina for its size.

The horse-loving Uzbeck tribe have bred up their Lokai horses with the use of southern breeds such as the Iomud and Karabair. Rich mountain pastures and selective breeding, based on natural aptitude for the rough, fast sport of 'goat snatching', has produced tough, sure-footed horses, equally useful for agriculture or harness, or for riding and toting packs on narrow, precipitous mountain trails. The Lokai stallions are in demand for improving other breeds in the south Tadjikistan.

The national sport of goat snatching certainly calls for strong, sure-footed horses, equally quick off the mark to gallop flat out and evade other riders trying to snatch the trophy, a dead goat. Karabair horses, like the Lokai, are often bred for the game, their speed showing the influence of long-dead Arab invaders' horses, their stamina being as great as that of the 'Mongols'.

Turkmene horses originate in that area between the Caspian Sea and Afghanistan called Turkmenistan and are more or less identical to the Persian Turkoman over the border. In each case the Akhal Teke is the most ancient and prized strain, believed by many to be the ancestor of the Arabian horse. These are the horses that provided the cavalry for King Darius of Persia, and took part in races 1000 to 2000 years B.C. They have long faces, with fine nostrils and expressive eyes. Their necks are long and thin, their head carriage characteristically high, their expression very alert. They have been known to cover 900 miles of waterless desert, and according to recent trials are only a little slower than Thoroughbreds. When Melekush, an Akhal Teke stallion, was presented to Queen Elizabeth in 1956, it left the other royal horses standing as they galloped up the wide grass verge of the Long Walk at Windsor Castle. This horse is now on loan to a lady rider, who delights in his gentle nature and his prowess at dressage and jumping.

In the Soviet Union, Akhal Tekes are bred at special collective farms and kept in 'tabuns' of ten to twelve mares per stallion, under the care of a herdsman. To those used to the rounded dimensions of most American breeds these horses

Akhal Teke

may appear at first as 'leggy' and uncomfortably narrow—but owners of Akhal Tekes acclaim them as being exceptional riding horses.

Iomud horses have the same origins, and poor strains are often improved with Akhal Teke blood. They have been evolved by an Iomud Turkoman tribe, but where the Akhal Teke is a desert horse, the Iomud comes from the steppes of northern Turkmenia, where the pasture has produced a slightly smaller and different type.

There are aristocratic Arabian horses in Russia called Strelets, named after the stud where they are bred. These horses, now breeding true, originated with selected native mares of the mountainous regions of the Ukraine, crossed with Turkish, Persian or principally, pure Arab sires, some of them supplied by the British Crabbet Park and Hungarian Babolna studs. The Terski, a true Arabian-type saddle horse, is bred in the North Caucasus, the product of Strelet sires used with pure-bred Arabian or Kabarda mares. Terskis now breed true, or are occasionally re-crossed with Arab, and show the characteristics of a large Arabian. The stallions are much used

Kabardin

for improving other breeds.

Trade between some Caucasians and Muslims of the Near East, resulted in well-bred, eastern-type stallions arriving in some Caucasus regions where they were mated with the local mares of Mongolian stock. The Kabardin breed which eventually ensued make first-class mountain horses. They have slightly convex profiles, long fine ears, and excellent legs and feet. Now largely crossed with Thoroughbreds, they are known as Anglo-Kabardins.

Most horses in southeastern Russia are of Mongolian origin. Many, like the Kustinair, were bred up by judicious crossing. This breed was improved with Don stallions, and they are now useful, hard harness and saddle horses of about 15 hands. Turkmenes were used to produce the Adayev strain.

The arduous work and harsh environment of the north Russian forests have produced several similar types of small, hardy, very shaggy horses, with layers of subcutaneous fat to withstand the winter's snow and frosts, and thick skins, impenetrable by the summer's hordes of insects. Despite mechanization, many horses are still used for the 'izvoz', transport of merchandise over snow-covered roads by sledge, and to haul timber deep in the forest.

The strong Viatka, 13 to 14 hands high, is particularly well known for its hardiness and good speed. It resembles the Polish Konik and bears traces of old Klepper blood. The Toric is one of the best-known working harness horses of the far north.

Two heavy breeds, the Lithuanian and the Latvian, are both based on small northern Zemaitukas and imported Finnish Drafts, with later crosses of Swedish Ardennes and Oldenburg. Latvians are known to have very equable temperaments.

The Russian Heavy Draft has a massive, muscular body combined with a lively nature. It originated from the native Ukrainian and was crossed with Ardennes, Percherons, Belgians and the Orlov Trotter. It is nearly a hand shorter than the

Viatka

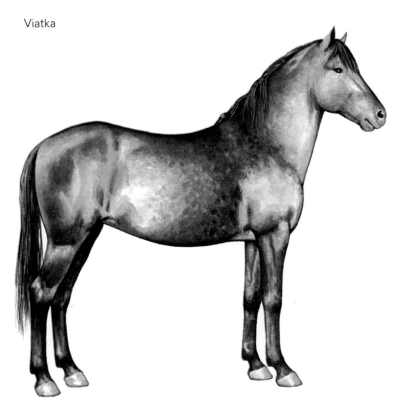

Lithuanian

15.3 Vladimir Heavy Draft, a well-made animal of mixed origins, including Cleveland Bays, Suffolks and Shires.

Racing is popular, and there are many studs of Thoroughbreds descended from imported animals. Trotting is also a favored sport, and the world famous Orlov Trotter is bred in large numbers, particularly at the Moscow State stud. This breed was the brain-child of Count Alexis Orlov, and was produced toward the end of the 18th century. The first stallion, an Arab, was crossed with a Dutch mare, and subsequent crossings were made with English Thoroughbred, Danish and Mecklenburg breeds, as well as additional Arab and Dutch. These handsome horses have 'Araby' heads and stand up to 17 hands. They were considered the fastest of all Trotters until the American Standardbred appeared on the scene. Now a very recent Orlov Standardbred cross, known as the Metis Trotter, promises to be the fastest yet. The Orlov-Rostopschiner is an excellent saddle horse.

A number of alien breeds are bred in the Soviet Union, and perhaps the most popular is the Trakehner. Those versatile and courageous horses that hailed from East Prussia are some which so many countries are finding the ideal animal for show-jumping and eventing.

Turkey

In 1620 the Malmesbury stud contained a Turkish mare. One school of thought contends it was therefore an Oriental type, probably with much Persian and Arab blood, and one of 'the best saddle horses in the world'.

General opinion would have it an Arabian mare, arguing that although the Turks have always been horse-minded, their horses were largely packhorse types; the so-called 'Turks' imported to England, were Arabians that arrived via the large area then called Turkey. Turkish Pashas collected large numbers of Arab horses by force or fraud—and bought them, as 'Turks', from the famous Arabian-producing Chrestowka stud. Small doubt but that the Byerley Turk, a progenitor of the English Thoroughbred, was an Arabian. Maybe it got its name because it was the one-time charger of Captain Byerley, who rode it at the Battle of the Boyne and supposedly captured his horse from the Turks at the siege of Buda. The Duke of Berwick imported the 'Lister Turk' during the reign of James II of England. The 'White Turk' and the 'Yellow Turk', both to sire stock that had much influence on horses famous in British racing, were imported between 1690 and 1700.

Turkey remains a land of horses, with more than a million used principally for farming, army remounts and for riding

Kurdistan half-bred

and draft. The native Kurdistan or Turkish ponies have short bodies and thick necks topped by common-looking heads. A popular Arab cross produces larger, faster, more refined ponies, that are both economical and useful.

When at the Royal Stud at Farahabad in Iran, I was shown a handsome gray, Oriental-type of riding horse, and was told it was a Jaf, a Kurdistan breed common to both Iran and Turkey. Possibly this was the 'best saddle horse in the world'. Karacabey horses are bred at the stud of that name. They are the most important breed, of good conformation and average 16 hands. They are used for cavalry and light draft work.

The Turkish Republic encourages horse breeding, and there are a number of State studs, some using Hungarian Nonius stallions to produce larger horses, some breeding pure Arabs as well as the local types.

Australasia

Australia

Horses were unknown on this continent until introduced by the first explorers from Spain or Holland in the 16th century. With the arrival of the British convict settlements and the opening up of the land to cattle and sheep, horses became a necessity.

Walers were being bred in New South Wales soon after the first settlement. The foundation stock came mostly from South Africa, Cape horses with origins steeped in Dutch and Spanish, Arab and Barb blood, with a later addition of Thoroughbred. They became famous as remounts for the Indian Army and during World War I. They come in many types, and are tough, fine horses, well known for riding and jumping, and their ability to buck. In 1968, Walers came first and second in the 100 mile endurance ride through the Blue Mountains. The first, claiming the Tom Quilty Gold Cup, was a stockhorse.

Today the units of mounted police, still found in most states, have shifted from their omnifarious, indispensable work in the outback, to traffic and crowd control in the cities. Instead of the heavy, weight-carrying animals of the trooper police, they ride quality horses, well-suited to public exhibitions of horsemanship and their many ceremonial duties.

Brumbies, the 'wild' horses that wander the bush in in-

Sydney Police Horse

creasing numbers, are a legacy of the gold rushes — when horse breeding was neglected and horses roamed the range, breeding at will, their progeny often 'scrub' animals that took to the wild. Brumbies are considered useless and, sadly, there is a scheme to reduce them by turning them into pet food.

Australians enthusiastically support all forms of racing, from the 'picnic races' of the outback to the celebrated Melbourne Cup, taking place each autumn. There are a growing number of first-class Thoroughbred studs, many blood animals being used not only for racing but for mustering on sheep or cattle stations, and even as pony club mounts. Numerous Arabian horses are bred, as well as European breeds.

Quarter horses were first imported in 1954. In 1967, Mr. Lougher set out from America with a shipment of thirty, to found another Australian stud. Because of hold-ups due to swamp fever regulations, his voyage eventually took 13 months and hit the world headlines. These horses are increasingly popular as stockhorses.

Sumba Pony

Indonesia

Ponies take pride of place in the groups of islands that make up Indonesia. They are indispensable for transport over the rough, roadless country, and the scant grazing keeps them, by natural selection, hardy, small and economical.

There were dancing horses in Persia hundreds of years before Christ, but they would have had to be very skilled to outdo the dancing ponies of Sumba. These stout little dorsal-striped, primitive types dance to the beat of tom-toms, with bells on their ankles, usually a small boy as a rider, and the directions conveyed via a lunge rope by their proud owners. The ponies' eyes seem to enlarge and glow as they 'give' to the rhythm of the contest, and marks are awarded for lightness and elegance.

The Sumbawa ponies are similar, and on both islands they are used in the popular sport of throwing the lance. These two islands also claim a better class, more valuable and larger type of pony called the Sandalwood—so named because Sumba's most important exports were ponies and sandalwood.

New Zealand
Like Australia, New Zealand has no indigenous horses and they were first imported toward the end of the 18th century. Much of the original stock came from Australia.

Thoroughbreds are raised and raced extensively, and many fine animals are produced, particularly those of island ancestry. Arabians are popular and are bred at various studs throughout the islands. The breed was introduced from India in the 1920's with later importations from the Crabbet Park Stud.

The native cow ponies are about 14.2 hands and usually crossbred. Some of them come from the large herds of feral horses, often of Thoroughbred blood, that belong to the Maoris but run wild in the Lake Taupo district. Their range and numbers have been affected by government afforestation projects, and since, unlike the Australian Brumbies, the New Zealand versions often make good stockhorses, numbers are caught for this purpose. The horses may be snared, herded into large stockyards or ridden down with relays of riders. They gradually catch up on one until it can be thrown and winded, by seizing its tail and galloping off at a tangent.

Africa

Once a year, four or five thousand horsemen converge on Churchill's 'Paris of the Sahara', Marakesh, for a *'charaga'* or tribal gathering. When their tents are pitched, outside the ancient, pink-tinted walls, they prepare for a *'fantassia'*—the exciting powder play that accompanies most feast days and celebrations throughout Morocco.

Around a thousand horsemen at a time gather in the arena, their horses decked out with red Morocco leather saddles and brightly colored wool saddle-cloths. They line up in contingents, and at a shout, thunder forward at the gallop awaiting the next command that sends them up in their stirrups, to wave and discharge their long *'mokkalas'* (muskets) in the air, while the horses plunge and the dust rises and the spectators yell with excitement. The charges are repeated again and again, and apparently help to ascertain the best of the horses and enhance their value greatly.

These horses are Barbs, fast, light animals with characteristically flat shoulders, long heads and low set tails, still as essential to everyday life in most parts of Morocco, Algeria and Libya as they were centuries ago. Supposed part descendants of the old Numidian horse, their origins are as obscure, and some say the same as those of the Arabian.

Many Barbs exported to England in days gone by were undoubtedly Arabians bred in Barbary, and a 'Barb' can also mean a horse from a barbaric, foreign country. They arrived in Spain with the Muslim invasions, had a great influence on the old Spanish Andalusians and, through them, numerous Continental and South American horses.

Comparatively few Barbs today are without Arabian blood, and the Libyan Barb is descended from a cross of the two breeds, plus traces of others brought in by the frequent migrations and invasions. Barbs are bred pure at a large stud at Constantine in Algeria.

Tsetse fly prohibits horses altogether in parts of Nigeria, but elsewhere they are mostly of Barb type. Before the devastating civil war of 1968, the heads of districts and villages used to ride to the capital of the Emirate to celebrate the Mohammedan Festival of Id-el-Fitre. They dressed their horses with decorated saddlery or quilted armor, those of Katsina and Bornu even wearing chain-mail, a relic of the Crusaders, and greeted their Emir with a spear brandishing charge, their horses pulled up on their haunches at the last possible moment.

A growing occupation with racing by the Kano traders

End of the Feast of Ramadan

during the 1930's brought interest in a heavier, stockier type of horse than the local Barbs. Roman-nosed Bahr-el-gazel, with powerful quarters and well set-on tails, arrived along the trade routes from the Sudan, past Lake Chad to Bornu, and proved good racers and heavy-type polo ponies.

Another, even less common type of horse is occasionally encountered in the Bornu district. It is a rangy, long-legged creature with a lengthy neck and back, poor quarters and a most pronounced Roman nose. It is known as the Bornu horse, or Dongola.

In Nigeria oxen are often employed for ploughing and carting, with camels and donkeys used as pack animals. Horses are for riding only, following on a slack rein behind a man on foot or another horse, or along the contours of the twisting track. Their heavy saddles, with high cantle and pommel, have flat wooden frames that make no concession for the curve of a horse's back and cause frequent sores, but fortunately the use of the severe old Arab bit has almost died out.

Fulani tribesmen, following the grazing trails with their flocks along the borders of Nigeria and the Cameroons, ride small, tough and hardy animals, which they also use for toting their belongings. These Fulani horses are of Oriental type but obviously have very mixed origins. Their ability to stand up to the rigors of their nomadic life are of considerably

153

Basuto Pony

greater importance to their Fulani owners than the manner in which they are bred.

The ability of a relatively few Dutch farmers in South Africa to withstand the might of the British Empire from 1899 to 1902 came as an incredible surprise to the whole world. But the British troops. mounted on unacclimatized, overweighted horses, weak from a long sea voyage, were quick to realize the main source of the Boers' strength. It lay with the sturdy little Basuto ponies they rode, the original Cape horses of fantastic stamina and Arabian, Barb and Persian blood, their beginnings going back to a handful of horses imported from Java in 1653 by the Dutch East India Company. Later additions of English roadster blood, and that of American-bred stallions and English Thoroughbreds, resulted in exactly the type of animal needed by the early settlers in their great treks inland from the Cape.

By the Boer War, Basuto ponies had been developed into fearless, sure-footed little horses that were accustomed to covering thirty or forty miles a day, moving at six miles an hour and carrying heavy equipment. On the march they were allowed to roll and graze for ten minutes in every hour. When they forbore to roll it was a signal they were too tired to be trekked further. When the reins were pulled over their heads and left on the ground, the ponies would stand un-attended; a system of 'ground-hitching' that added to the Boers' fire-power, by releasing the one man in four needed by the British troops for horse holding.

Because the veld was their own familiar homeland, the Boers were able to rest and graze their horses by day, their commandos moving quickly by night to harass the troops. The high reputation of the animals they rode remains, even though true Basuto ponies—first acquired in Basutoland around 1822 by Zulu raiding—are hard to come by today.

It is impossible to leave Africa without mentioning Egyptian horses and the high-class desert Arabians, bred for many years in the good climatic conditions of the El Zahraa and Ein Shams studs.

Egyptian Arab

BOOKS TO READ

Horses. George Gaylord Simpson. Doubleday, 1961.

The Horse of the Desert. W. R. Brown. Macmillan, 1947.

"The Story of the Horse" by W. H. Carter. *National Geographic Magazine*, vol. 44, 1923, pp. 455-566.

The Horse of the Americas. R. M. Denhardt. University of Oklahoma Press, 1947.

Our Equine Friends. W. Dinsmore and J. Harvey. Horse and Mule Association of America, 1944.

The Horse: A Study in Natural History. W. H. Flower. D. Appleton, 1892.

Our American Horse. D. C. Hogner. Thomas Nelson and Sons, 1944.

The Horse. R. F. Meysey-Thompson. London: Edward Arnold, 1911.

The Origin and Influence of the Thoroughbred Horse. W. Ridgeway. Cambridge, England: University Press, 1905.

"Breeds of Light Horses" by H. H. Reese. U. S. Department of Agriculture, Farmers' Bulletin No. 952, 1918.

The Horseman's Encyclopedia. M. C. Self. Barnes, 1946.

"The Ascent of Equus" by C. Stock and H. Howard. Los Angeles County Museum Science Series, No. 8, 1944.

The Horse in History. B. Tozer. London: Methuen, 1908.

The History and Romance of the Horse. Arthur Vernor. Boston: Waverly House, 1939.

The Wild Horse of the West. Walker D. Wyman. Caldwell: Caxton Printers, 1946.

Meet the Horse. Patricia H. Johnson. Grosset & Dunlap, 1967.

Select, Buy, Train, Care for Your Own Horse. Barbara Van Tuyl. Grosset & Dunlap, 1967.

The Quarter Horse. Walter D. Osborne. Grosset & Dunlap, 1967.

The Horse in The West. Bradley Smith. World, 1969.

Complete Book of Horses. Howard J. Lewis. Random House, 1957.

Know about Horses: a ready reference guide to horses, horse people and horse sports. Harry Disston. Devin-Adair, 1961.

Your Horse: his selection, stabling and care. George C. Saunders. Van Nostrand, 1966.

A Horse of Your Own. M. A. Stoneridge. Doubleday, 1968.

The American Horse. Barney Nagler. Macmillan, 1966.

The Horse in America. Robert West Howard. Follett, 1965.

The Horse America Made: the story of the American Saddle Horse. Louis Taylor. Harper, 1961.

INDEX

OTHER TITLES IN THE SERIES

The GROSSET ALL-COLOR GUIDES provide a library of authoritative information for readers of all ages. Each comprehensive text with its specially designed illustrations yields a unique insight into a particular area of man's interests and culture.

NOW AVAILABLE

SOON TO BE PUBLISHED